Worshipology

A biblical, practical, and spiritual guide to living and leading worship

Kurtis Parks

Worshipology: A biblical, pratical, and spiritual guide to living and leading worship
www.worshipologybook.com
www.kurtisparks.com

Copyright © 2022 by Kurtis Parks

Published by The Core Media Group, Inc., www.thecoremediagroup.com.
The author is represented by WordServe Literary Group, Ltd., www.wordserveliterary.com.

Cover Design: Riley Flynn
Interior Design: Nadia Guy

ISBN 978-1-950465-60-6

Printed in the United States of America.

Contents

This book is dedicated to my kids, Norah and Moses. While I hope to inspire and challenge many leaders to deeper levels of worship, you two are my most prized students. Discipling you in the ways of Jesus is my greatest calling. I love you guys so much and you are my best buddies. You are the reason I believe there's a generation of true worshipers rising up. The way you worship Jesus and sing your praise makes my eyes water and heart fill. I continuously pray that God shapes you into the leaders of the future and that you always live with the heart of worship of David.

Scan the QR code for a special prayer from KP as you start this book.

Genesis Moments

We all have a genesis moment. A moment when something new begins inside of us and we start our journey toward our purpose. When God's voice meets our prayers and we start to see through the fog of life a little clearer. This is one of the most amazing things about a life in Christ—we all get a do-over, or as Jesus said in John 3:3, we get to be born again. It's a new story beginning with a new chapter. A genesis moment, as I call it, is when the spark of purpose is lit. It's Moses at the burning bush, or Abraham beneath the starry skies. It's Peter and Andrew on the beach hearing the words "Come and follow me" spoken by a carpenter from Nazareth. A genesis moment is what changed the trajectory of my life when I was in middle school.

When I was 11 years old, living in Panama City, Florida, my lifelong road of leading worship was at the starting line. My dad heard me singing Disney songs around the house and I must've been on key, because he asked me to be his worship leader. Our family was in the early stages of planning a move to Virginia, where my dad would plant a church. I couldn't play an instrument, I didn't know what a chord chart was, and I certainly had never led a band before. Call it a prophetic word, but that moment of fatherly recognition led to my lifelong pursuit of the heart of worship, helping people connect to God's presence, and a quest for musical excellence. On that particular day it wasn't just my dad's voice; it was the Holy Spirit speaking through him, calling me to something that would change my life. Much like God using Samuel to call out the potential in a scrappy shepherd boy named David, this was my genesis moment.

It started with my parents enrolling me in piano lessons. Of course, like many 11-year-olds, the last thing I wanted to do was practice piano. I wanted to be playing street hockey, building forts, and trading baseball cards. So my dad, the genius that he was, told me that if I practiced for an hour every day, he would pay me $10 a week. That got my attention! I plinked away on the piano, and eventually after about a year of "Chopsticks" and "Heart and Soul," I got to where I was halfway decent. In my second year, I started writing originals, and by the time I was 13, I was singing and playing simultaneously. It was then that I made the biggest mistake of my childhood—I told my parents they didn't have to pay me anymore. I could've gotten so many more Benjamins! Or at least Madisons. Nevertheless, I had gotten to a place where I enjoyed playing piano, I liked the sounds coming out, and I actually looked forward to sitting down and practicing my craft. When I was 14, my family made the move to Roanoke, Virginia, where my dad planted a church. And yes, you guessed it: I started leading worship. I always thought it was because I was free labor and a cheap staff member to keep around, but I know now there was more to it.

My dad saw a diamond in the rough, and trust me, in the beginning days of leading worship, rough is an understatement. I'm just glad smartphones didn't exist back then because I'm sure those first couple of years had some worship services that would have gone viral on YouTube, and not due to immense talent! I had no idea what I was doing. Neither did much of the band, but I quickly started to figure out how to connect with musicians. I studied seasoned worship leaders, watched live concerts, and hung out with people who were further along in their leadership and musicianship. Much like getting in a gym and hiring a trainer, I wanted to be around people who would make me better.

The first "trainer" I had was Scott. He moved with us to start our church plant, and he let me lead worship alongside him for the first year. He was a songwriter and a gifted guitarist. We didn't just hang out onstage on Sundays; we did life with one another! I mean that literally, because he actually lived with us in our basement. He showed me songs he was working on, we listened to the latest Vineyard albums (which I still listen to), and taught me the ways of music theory. A year into starting our church, and for reasons I can't remember, Scott moved away, and a lady named Janet moved into that leader/mentor role. I learned about other styles, first heard Gospel music, and grew a ton under her leadership.

But once more, she moved on as people often do, and soon afterward I was put in charge of the worship team. Without those years of coaching, I don't know if I would have made it. While Scott showed me the ropes in chord progressions and songwriting, he didn't have much background in leading worship and pastoring people. Janet showed me how to relate to others and make it about Jesus. I quickly realized as a teenager leading a church in musical worship that there is a lot more to leading worship than just picking songs and leading a band on Sunday. I write this book for the new worship leaders and musicians who might not have a coach like Scott or a mentor like Janet and who are looking for a baseline to build from. I think if I'd had a manual of some sort back then, I would have gotten off to a much stronger start. So, thanks for letting me be your Scott, and through the pages on this book, we can hang out for a while and talk shop.

Passion

So many people use the word "passion" for what they really enjoy. But one of the most accurate definitions of "passion" is "suffering." What are you willing to suffer for? Whether your passion is music or jogging, it will require sacrifice. So what are you willing to lay down for your passion? For Jesus, He was willing to go to the cross for us. That's the story of *the* passion. Whatever your passion is, you will do what you have to do in order to see it become a reality.

By that definition, I wouldn't really say food is my passion, but I can say that I'm pretty obsessed with grilling. I grill out on my deck five or six days a week, rain or shine. At a recent worship team hangout, I was grilling burgers for the worship team and it literally started hailing! Burgers, chicken, salmon, pork chops—you name it, I grill it. I love to barbecue. It's my contribution to the high-quality cooking lineage I have. My grandparents were from Czechoslovakia and made native dishes that would make your mouth water. My mom is a published cookbook author and still makes some of the tastiest desserts every holiday season. And my wife, Sarah, is a master in the kitchen. So I try to hold my own on a grill. I watch *Beat Bobby Flay* as a student, learning new tricks of the trade. And I have to admit, I'm pretty good.

But I didn't just learn the ways of a grill master from a book or from watching a bunch of shows on the Food Network. I got around great grillers! My father-in-law, Pete, taught me everything I know. He is a true Yoda when it comes to grilling and smoking meats. Every time I visit, he shows me how he preps the food, the right temperatures to cook at, how long to cook. It's truly an art form. I continually want to learn, and somewhere down deep inside, I believe I'll be a contestant on *Iron Chef*. Who knows, maybe some day I'll open my own restaurant. I'm soaking up every nugget of knowledge I can get right now when I'm around Pete. He's patient with me, and I think he actually gets more excited teaching me how to cook than I do.

That's what happens when you pour out your cup. It refills you. When it comes to leading worship, I've become more of a mentor these days than a protégé. I don't know if that's just me getting older or the fact that I've made so many mistakes onstage that I could write a book about it (and I did!). I'll never stop learning, so in some ways I'll always be a student; but I feel called to pour out what I've learned these last 25 years as a worship leader, and more so as a worship pastor. The point is, a book won't answer every question. This book isn't the finish line. It's a starting line. So, yes, read and learn, but also get around others who are doing what you want to do. Get around others who are where you want to be! Build relationships that will challenge you.

The disciples didn't just read about Jesus or watch YouTube videos on how to do life-transforming ministry. They got around Jesus. They saw what He did, heard what He said, and then they did it. Community trumps knowledge every time. *Knowledge informs, but community transforms.* You have to get around others who are where you want to be. Surround yourself with better musicians, coaches, and pastors who can pour what they have into you. Find a mentor and open your mind and heart up to learning everything you can. Grab coffee with a gifted songwriter if you want to start writing songs. Maybe do a Zoom call with a seasoned worship leader! There is no ego when it comes to growth. We'll talk about that later.

Do what you can to grow, and then put it into practice. I think that when you study alone it's great, but when you practice in community, it's even better. To know any subject well, you have to become a student of that subject. Long before Beethoven wrote his masterful symphonies, he studied under Haydn and Salieri. Long before Michelangelo sculpted "David," he was an apprentice to Ghirlandaio. And long before Peter and James pastored churches in the time of Acts, they studied under the Great Teacher, Jesus.

I write this book to be a biblical, practical, and spiritual guide to anyone involved in leading worship. We need all three of those approaches to be well rounded and equipped to lead. A few years ago I wrote a book called *Sound Check* about pursuing authenticity, purpose, and excellence in our worship experiences and leadership. After writing the book, I did a series of videos on YouTube called "Worshipology," and that inspired the idea to write this book. I'm taking some of the concepts we covered in those short video blogs and expanding on them here. At the time I wrote *Sound Check* I was the worship director at National Community Church, based out of Washington, DC. It's been a joy to hear worship leaders and teams go through that book and grow together in their understanding and passion to lead congregational worship.

As I write this, my family and I have just gone through a season of planting Bridges Nashville, a start-up church that meets downtown in Music City, teaching through worship. Our service is styled sort of like a VH1 *Storytellers* episode, where we combine story and scripture with song. I preach in a TED Talk style, with messages designed to be 20 minutes or less. If you haven't figured out by now, I'm pretty ADD in my thought process but conversational in my writing style. Recent studies show that the average attention span is less than 12 minutes, so I figured that instead of fighting it, I would lean into it. Even with the most gifted speakers on the planet, it's hard for me to sit through an hour-long sermon. Plus, if I can read the Sermon on the Mount in less than 15 minutes, I'm positive it didn't take Jesus too long to deliver it. I also learned that a goldfish has an attention span of 9 seconds. You're welcome.

The other unique part of our service at Bridges is what we call *selah*. As you probably guessed, it comes out of Psalms. The closest definition we have for that word is to "pause and reflect," so that's what we do. We have our bands play instrumentally, with encouraging scriptures on the screens, and our prayer team available on the sides of the sanctuary. It's a time in our service when we can meditate on whatever God is doing in that moment. People often open their Bibles; others just sit with their eyes closed, meditating in His presence. The Spirit moves powerfully in that time, and funny enough, many people say it's their favorite part of the service. I have no doubt that music exists in heaven, and there are moments when we get to join heaven's song here on Earth. God's presence has a soundtrack, and it's called worship.

There's honestly no better way to get the gospel into people's hearts than through a song. In my role as a pastor, God has taught me so many things that I never was tuned into when my world was completely focused on musical worship. I've been driven to my knees in prayer and to my desk in study. There's a hunger that grows exponentially when you catch a fire to know the God of worship and not just experience the power of worship. The more I know, the more I realize how little I know, which just keeps me grounded and hungry. As my pastor Mark Batterson would always say, "Stay hungry and stay humble and there's nothing God can't do in and through you!"

I hope these pages inspire you to dive deeper into the Word and into the presence of God. That's what worship is all about: knowing the heart of the Father. This world doesn't need another great song, another great band, another great speaker, or even another great church. We need more of God's presence. Our vision statement at Bridges Nashville is simple: to be a place where God's presence and His people connect. As worship leaders, we get a front seat to witness His presence change lives every week. When we have churches filled with people who are hungry for His presence, that's when our cities and our communities start to change. My heart in writing is to see all of us closer to Jesus. If the only time we lead worship is with a microphone in front of us, then we're living a lie. We can't let the only time we spend with God be in a professional setting. Let's be a people of His presence, and disciple our teams to be better lovers of Jesus.

I've heard it said that alone you go fast, but together you go far. So in that spirit, I've asked some of the most spirit-filled, kingdom-minded worship leaders I know to contribute to this book in a special way. Each chapter ends with a "closing thought" from worship leaders across the board. Some are well known, others you may have never heard of, but God knows each one by name, and I'm honored to call them friends. So let's get a little closer to Jesus through each of these chapters. Let's know Him so that we can know ourselves and help others know Him more. Let's jump into the study of worship, or as I like to call it, "Worshipology."

CHAPTER 1

Worship Teachers

Audio Technology with Mr. Duncan was my favorite class in college. Twice a week we studied and practiced the methods behind recording music. We learned which microphones to use, how to set them up, the proper technique of wrapping cables (and every production volunteer said "amen"). We talked about choosing the right preamp, using software, and all the bells and whistles that come with a recording studio. The best part about the class was that students could book studio time and work on projects as part of the learning experience. Many late nights were spent there, filled with energy drinks, good friends, and delirious studio sessions.

During that year, I was so inspired that I got my first recording system, a Tascam Portastudio, which is now considered vintage and by all accounts obsolete. What cost me a month of my pizza delivery salary at the time you can now buy for under $200! Yet, here I am years later, writing this chapter from my home studio in Nashville. My gear has gotten better throughout the years, and I've spent way too much money on software. But the methods and techniques I learned in that class have guided me along the way. What I learned from Mr. Duncan helped me make a career out of music. These days I have the joy of working with other young producers and passing on the tricks of the trade I've learned over the last 15 years of making records. Once a student, now a teacher—that's the goal of growth in any field, including worship leading. It's also the goal of discipleship.

Jesus walked with His disciples, not just to feed them but also to teach them to feed themselves and others. Right before He ascended to the right hand of the Father, Jesus gave His followers the Great Commission:

> Therefore go and make disciples of all nations, baptizing them in the name of the Father and of the Son and of the Holy Spirit, and teaching them to obey everything I have commanded you. And surely I am with you always, to the very end of the age. (Matt. 28:19-20)

Teach the world what I have taught you! People can't learn what they don't know without a teacher. And as the disciples became apostles, they passed on their firsthand experiences with Jesus and lived out His commands to start the early Acts church!

Not long after, we meet a man named Paul who becomes an apostle himself and plants churches all across the ancient landscape. Paul knew the value of teaching others and passed on his passion and knowledge to younger minds like Timothy and Titus. Jesus had disciples, then His disciples made disciples. It's the circle of life—the Jesus life! In both Jesus and Paul we see the importance of protégés. I was once a protégé, and now I spend most of my time as a mentor. It doesn't mean you ever stop learning, but at some point you need to pour out what you've been filled with!

Paul also knew the value of music and saw it as a way to influence culture and teach an unbelieving world about the kingdom of God. In two different letters to new churches, Paul told them to teach through the method of—wait for it.... —music! To the Colossians he wrote,

> Let the message of Christ dwell among you richly as you teach and admonish one another with all wisdom through psalms, hymns, and songs from the Spirit, singing to God with gratitude in your hearts. (Col. 3:16)

To the Ephesians he wrote,

> . . . speaking to one another with psalms, hymns, and songs from the Spirit. Sing and make music from your heart to the

Lord, always giving thanks to God the Father for everything, in the name of our Lord Jesus Christ. (Eph. 5:19-20)

Learning Through Song

Teaching through song has roots in the Old Testament. Moses wrote songs to tell of God's faithfulness that the future generations would sing and remember. Just like the physical monuments the Israelites built at Jordan and other places where miracles occurred, songs were monuments that lived in the people's hearts. The psalms are a great example of spiritual mementos that went on to teach people through the ages the message of an all-powerful God. **"Let this be written for a future generation, that a people not yet created may praise the LORD" (Ps. 102:18).**

Think back on moments in your own life when songs taught you different things. We learn our ABCs as a song. Maybe you remember the song about the state capitals? Nursery rhymes teach stories that have lasted for hundreds of years. It might seem hard to memorize a script, but when you put words to music, the brain starts to work at a quicker pace. When the Bible is put to melody, it finds its way into the depths of our souls. When I was a kid, we grew up on Steve Green's "Hide 'Em in Your Heart" series. His songs taught me verses like Ephesians 6:1 (Children Obey Your Parents) and Matthew 19:14 (Let the Little Children Come). To be honest, decades later I can still recite most of those albums from heart. And that's exactly where memory keeps the Scriptures—in your heart! Music + Message = Memory.

Did you know that music has been proven to help Alzheimer's patients remember events, places, and people in their lives? Music therapy is a growing occupation, and we even have a couple of students in our church who are taking classes in college to become music therapists. I love the movie *The King's Speech*, which tells the story of King George VI becoming king of England. He has a major speech impediment but ends up working with a speech therapist who uses unconventional techniques to help the king overcome his public-speaking challenge. In one scene Lionel Logue, the king's speech aid, puts a pair of headphones on the king and asks King George to recite Shakespeare. The music worked its magic, and he was able to say the entire passage without a single stutter.

When we connect the Word of God to the worship of God, it makes its way into the people of God. Paul told the early church to use the method of song to carry the message of Christ. At a time when Bibles weren't sold in bookstores or available for a free download on smart phones, singing Scripture was a way to remember.

As worship leaders, we have the opportunity to not just lead songs but also to pastor people. Part of that privilege is teaching through worship. Let me say here that you can't teach what you don't know. In Colossians 3 it first says to "let the message of Christ dwell among you" before it says to "teach and admonish one another." If we want to educate others with the Scriptures through song, we need to first be students of the Bible. Get into the Word of God so that the Word gets into you.

I'll never forget being at a conference where my friend Aaron Keyes was leading worship. He was dropping Bible verses left and right before going into songs, tying together Word and worship like a spider weaves a web. It was incredible to see that type of leadership. It inspired me to go to another level in my Bible reading. Since that moment I've read through the Bible every year, with various reading plans thanks to the YouVersion app. The amazing thing about the Bible is that it always has something fresh to say, and every time you open the Scriptures, God opens His mouth. The writer of Hebrews says it like this: "For the word of God is alive and powerful. It is sharper than the sharpest two-edged sword, cutting between soul and spirit, between joint and marrow. It exposes our innermost thoughts and desires." Sometimes we read the Bible, but most of the time the Bible reads us! Develop a hunger for the Word and you'll find that the more you study, the more you'll be able to teach.

Storytellers

The next time you are preparing to lead a worship service, look at the lyrics of your set list through the lens of Scripture. What are the songs saying, and where in the Bible are they drawing inspiration from? You have a chance to be a storyteller. You may or may not remember VH1's *StoryTellers*, but it was always a favorite TV show of mine. Bands and artists would perform a concert, in front of a smaller audience, and share the stories behind some of their biggest songs. On one episode the Goo Goo Dolls were the guests (one of my all-time favorite bands), and John Rzeznik was masterfully sharing the stories behind their songs. Fans got a glimpse not only of the artists' personalities but also of their hearts, and they heard the deep truths behind the hits they'd come to know from radio. After sharing stories, the band would kick into the song. It was amazing to see people's reactions to a song after hearing the story behind it.

It happens in worship too. Before leading a song like Chris Tomlin's "Our God," you could share Romans 8:31: "If our God is for us, who can be against us." The beautiful thing that happens is that people make the connection that worship songs aren't just cool lyrics put to nice melodies but are filled with the living and active Word of God. So on a Tuesday, when someone from your church is going through a hard time and they begin to hum the worship song from Sunday, they can recall the verse that you shared just before leading it. They might make a beeline to their Bible to read the rest of that chapter and head down a rabbit trail of God's grace through His Word.

See, one of my main goals as a pastor is to inspire people to open their Bibles every day. I want them to discover for themselves the truth hidden in the pages. Just like I can't spoon-feed my children forever, I can't read your Bible for you. And I can't worship for you. You have to do that yourself. Every time we help someone learn how to worship God on their own, we are carrying out the Great Commission—teaching and making disciples.

Let's go back to the New Testament instruction about teaching through song to the early church in Colossians 3:16. Paul wrote this letter from a prison cell, which tells us just how important it was to get it out. Nothing would stop the message from reaching the Church! This is such a rich verse that I think it deserves to be dissected so it can be properly digested. Let's take a closer look.

Teach and Admonish

Think about your favorite schoolteacher. They were probably someone who illuminated the subject matter in a way that made it come alive. They inspired and challenged you to learn and grow. The same is true with our pastors. They help shed a light on the character of God, the ways of Jesus, the power of the Holy Spirit, and the depth of Scripture. Teaching is a skill, and if you want to do it, it's worth doing well. When you're preparing for a church service, dive into the Bible to connect the dots. What is the journey of worship that you are taking your church on during that service? In the book *The Art of Curating Worship*, Mark Pierson writes about worship as not just a song set but as an event to curate. Just like an art curator would display a piece and tell the story behind it, we can do so in our times of musical worship. A curator would ask the following questions about a piece of art, and we can ask the same questions about the songs we are leading:

• What stands out to you from this painting?
• What moment in the story has been captured?
• What was the artist wanting the people of his or her day to understand about the story?
• If you were the artist, what moment in the story would you want to capture?
• Why that part?

Study the song and the message behind it. Write out what you want to say, and then say it out loud in your house before you share it in front of your church. This is more on the practical side of things, but you want to be clear in what you're teaching so that it doesn't come out confusing. There's nothing worse than trying to get a point across that no one can understand. Before I ever preach a message on Sunday, I've preached it a dozen times to myself and my family, even recording it sometimes to listen to, making sure it comes out clearly, confidently, and with conviction. If I can't get excited about what I'm going to share, how can I expect anyone else to? If I don't believe what I'm going to speak, how can I desire that in others? Let your passion for Jesus come out as you teach. It's okay to have a personality, as long as you don't make it about you.

I've heard people say that stage presence isn't something for the worship world. I have to disagree. Jesus had the X factor, and people were drawn to Him. If Jesus had been boring, I don't know that crowds would have shown up. He had charisma and was inspiring, because He carried the hope of the world. If we're to follow in His footsteps, let's do so with a holy energy. Practicing a teaching moment in the safety of your home also lets you work on your timing. You've heard it said that timing is everything. I would encourage you to share a thought, not a sermon, before a song. Don't feel like you have to share a 30-minute message on the theology behind the book of Revelation before leading

"Revelation Song" by Jennie Lee Riddle. Maybe share a brief passage and a simple idea behind it. For instance, with this song I would probably share Revelation 4:8: "Day and night they never stop saying: 'Holy, holy, holy is the Lord God Almighty,' who was, and is, and is to come." I might then explain, "When we worship God together in a corporate setting, we are a mirror image of what happens around the clock in heaven. The only response to an almighty God is to sing 'Holy Holy Holy,' so let's do that now with this next song."

Paul also tells us to admonish one another in Colossians 3:16. "Admonish" translates as a warning, counsel, and encouragement or exhortation. Warning might sound harsh, but think about this: a warning is always out of care for someone. A stop sign is a warning for people to keep them from having a car accident. An allergy warning on a food item is to keep people safe from experiencing an allergic reaction. A warning is always done from a spirit of kindness and consideration. Encouraging is a huge piece of admonishing. Teaching should never be done from a "holier than thou" perspective. It should be done with a humble heart, in grace and love, to see others built up and grow in their faith.

With All Wisdom

If we are going to teach, we must do it with wisdom. There's nothing worse than sharing a passage of Scripture and finding out afterwards that it didn't mean what you thought it did. Or finding out that you quoted the wrong passage. Always double-check that you've got the right verse. I learned this lesson the hard way, and I have a permanent reminder. I'm a fan of tattoos and have them all over my arms, with Scripture as the theme tying them all together. When my son was born I went to get a tattoo commemorating his life verse, Exodus 15:2. It says, "The LORD is my strength and my song; he has given me victory. This is my God, and I will praise him—my father's God, and I will exalt him!" The artwork around it was so amazing that I didn't pay attention to the verse that the tattoo artist actually tattooed on my arm. It was Exodus 15:12: "You raised your right hand, and the earth swallowed our enemies." I mean, that's a pretty cool verse, but it's not exactly what I had in mind. Fortunately we were able to add some elements and correct the tattoo, but nevertheless, check your reference point!

This is why study is so important. "Work hard so you can present yourself to God and receive his approval. Be a good worker, one who does not need to be ashamed and who correctly explains the word of truth (2 Tim. 2:15). Correctly explain the Word. This is where context and content come into play. Context is understanding the scripture's background, who wrote it, and why it was written. You can check the Greek language for New Testament passages, or Hebrew with Old Testament verses. I love finding out the depth of a word by going to the original language. Knowing the context is crucial. You also have to know *your* context. If you're leading a youth service filled with teenagers, don't share something over their heads or experiences that they can't relate to.

What are you trying to say, and does it make sense? For instance, if I'm going to lead a song that talks about battles, warfare, or being in the midst of a storm, I have to think about who might be present in the service. A first-time church attender might bolt for the door if they hear a song about war or being in the "army of the Lord." If you sing "this is how I fight my battles" without any explanation, you could have a lot of head scratching in your congregation. However, if you take a moment to share a passage that clarifies the metaphor, it will go a long way.

I remember the first time I led "The Lion and the Lamb" and one of my pastor friends encouraged me to take a second to explain those references. It never dawned on me before that to someone who didn't grow up in church, it could sound like we're worshiping animals. Think of the lyrics you're leading, and understand that there are songs that might need a little unwrapping. Plenty of worship songs are written from a poetic standpoint, but not everyone is a poet. Metaphors give you an opportunity to teach, so be sure to do it with wisdom. Speaking of wisdom, if you're newer to this idea of "teaching moments," it's never a bad idea to run a teaching moment by a pastor or another church leader who you respect. They could bring a different perspective and help you grow in your leadership and understanding!

Psalms, Hymns, and Spirit Songs

Paul gives us three categories of music to teach with. The first is the book of Psalms, which I will jump into at length in another chapter. However, we know that psalms are the foundation of many modern-day worship songs. These are some of the simplest ways you can share a teaching moment. Before leading a song like "Better is One Day" by Matt Redman, you could simply share the passage from Psalm 84. Before leading "Great Are You, Lord" by All Sons and Daughters, you could share a quick reading from Psalm 145. You can also utilize the psalms as a call to worship before singing the first song. We often open up our services at Bridges Nashville with a short reading from Psalms. Here are several examples:

- Psalm 96:1—"Sing a new song to the LORD! Let the whole earth sing to the LORD!"
- Psalm 100:4—"Enter his gates with thanksgiving and his courts with praise; give thanks to him and praise his name."
- Psalm 145:3—"Great is the LORD! He is most worthy of praise! No one can measure his greatness."
- Psalm 150:1—"Praise the LORD. Praise God in his sanctuary; praise him in his mighty heavens."

The psalms are also helpful in teaching the posture of praise. We will talk about the seven Hebrew words for praise in another chapter, with all of those words appearing in the psalms as different ways to physically express praise. I've used Psalm 63:4 to teach why we raise our hands in worship and have referenced Psalm 95:6 to explain the act of bowing down in worship. There's no limit to using the psalms to teach in worship!

Hymns are a portal to a world of theology. I admit that I grew up without knowing a single hymn, other than "Amazing Grace," and that's just because I heard it at a funeral. In the last decade or so, I've fallen in love with this genre and have even reworked dozens of hymns to give them a modern sound, while maintaining the integrity of the original work. It's been fun to breathe new life into songs that are centuries old and see them connect with a new generation. Hymns are filled with lyrics and melodies of the past written by some of the most devoted Christ-followers. Sharing the stories behind the songs and the songwriters is a powerful way to honor the tradition and history of the church.

Fanny Crosby is one such songwriter. Incredibly she wrote more than 9,000 hymns! She was the first woman to speak in the Senate, she was blind most of her life, and she started every songwriting session with prayer. Then you have the Wesley brothers, who wrote as a team. One brother would be preaching at the front of the church while the others were in the back turning sermon notes into lyrics. Sharing stories behind hymns connects generations through testimony.

I'm always inspired when I learn the background of a hymn. "The Old Rugged Cross" was written in 1912 by George Bennard. Introduced at a Chicago convention with the famous preacher Billy Sunday, the song immediately became popular and made its way across the U.S. Bennard wrote the song as a response to ridicule that he'd received at a revival. He wanted to tell the story of redemption through the power of the cross. "Amazing Grace" was written by John Newton, a slave-trading seaman who had his life turned around by Jesus. He went on to be a leading voice in abolishing slavery in the UK, alongside William Wilberforce. The hymn "It Is Well" was written by Horatio Spafford, who discovered by telegram that all four of his daughters had died at sea. He penned the words on a ship crossing over the very place where his girls lost their lives.

Hymns often contain a powerful lyric that you could dive into as a teaching moment. A line like "born to raise the sons of earth, born to give them second birth" from the classic Christmas hymn "Hark the Herald Angels Sing" could be a beautiful teaching moment about the reconciliation and redemption found in Christ. If you don't gravitate toward singing hymns in your church, I would encourage you to give it a try. Maybe try a modern version of a hymn. We have thousands of hymns as part of our worship heritage, and they have made a rapid resurgence in more recent years.

Songs of the Spirit, or Spirit songs, are the more mysterious part of Paul's passage. Coming from a more charismatic background, I can offer my thoughts on what he's referencing, but I also encourage you to dive into Scripture and discover the meaning for yourself. I believe the Holy Spirit inspires us in the moment. "For at that time the Holy Spirit will teach you what you should say" (Luke 12:12).

If you ask to be filled with the Spirit of God, don't be surprised when He fills you not only with power but also with song! When we make ourselves available to be used as His instruments, the Holy Spirit can speak to us and through us. There have been more moments than I can recall when spontaneous praise filled the room and a song was born out of that time. There are also times when I have been leading a song and

I felt a certain impression to sing out a line continuously so that the message could linger. There are also songs of the Spirit that have come from our times of *selah* at Bridges Nashville when our band has started a musical interlude and spontaneous lyrics are sung in the moment *for* the moment. There is no greater teacher than the Holy Spirit, who gives perfect wisdom and discernment. I believe songs of the Spirit can happen just as much in the quiet of your home as they can in a larger gathering. Seventeenth-century friar Brother Lawrence taught the idea of "practicing the presence of God." I believe the more time you spend in God's presence, the more songs of the Spirit will make their way into your heart.

Share the Story

Jesus taught through stories. We know them as parables, but they're really just stories relatable to that culture and people. Jesus taught about the Kingdom and the gospel in metaphors that people could understand. Just as you can share a psalm, hymn, or song of the Spirit to teach and admonish others in worship, you can also share a story or a testimony to teach. Many of the songs we lead and sing every weekend have powerful origins to them. I love that more and more artists are creating "song story" videos to go beyond the music and tell the heart of the song. Sometimes we'll share these testimonies before leading a song.

"Raise a Hallelujah" by Jonathan and Melissa Helser is a great example. The song was written as a prayer for a young boy in the hospital fighting for his life. "How He Loves" by John Mark McMillan was written from a place of pain and suffering after the death of his best friend. It was a conversation he had with God that so many can relate to. That song has been a healing song for many people walking through their own tragedies. You can share what a particular song has meant to you personally as a teaching moment mixed with testimony. Remember, according to Revelation 12:11, we overcome by the blood of the Lamb (that's what Jesus did for everyone) and by the word of our testimony (that's what Jesus did in *your* life).

Some songs connect to seasons in our lives that will help others through their current storms. Whenever I sing the anthem "10,000 Reasons," it takes me back to a place where I was stepping into a new role as a worship pastor, discipling a new team, and teaching a new church the heart of worship. That song was an anchor for me during a chaotic time when I felt unqualified and in over my head. Today when I lead it, I remind people that there are too many reasons to list to praise God. He's the answer for every question and the solution to every problem in our lives.

Every song has a story. Learn the scriptures and stories that songs spring out of, and then teach and admonish the Church through them. Remember, we don't just lead songs; we get to lead people.

Closing Thought

Bible college didn't prepare me to lead worship. I figured that as long as I had a great band, stayed on the click, and played the latest CCLI hits, the people of God would be lost in the anointing I was bringing. Suffice it to say, I was in for a rude awakening.

Every weekend, every service, every transition, and every worship moment is an opportunity to teach about worship—because the call of a worship leader isn't just to sing songs and manage the excellence of a band. It's to give voice to the people of God. Our job is not to discover our own voice under the lights and on a stage. It's to help the Church find her voice, declaring the promises and greatness of God.

But my understanding of corporate worship never brought me beyond the mechanical excellence of preparing songs. Don't get me wrong. We prepared our hearts. We prayed like our lives depended on it. We did devos. We made sure our hearts were focused. But what was missing was truly pastorally helping the church to sing—to discover her identity as the Bride of Christ. Before that, I was simply playing songs for people, hoping they'd be inspired to enter in.

But our job is to shine a spotlight upon the glory of God and get out of the way. Worship teams exist to help people sing, and then we must fade into the background of a radiant Savior, worthy of all praise, honor, glory, and full attention. So don't be content to just prepare songs. Lead people. Love people. Relate. Engage. Help the Church to sing.

David Santistevan
Worship leader and songwriter
Founder, "Beyond Sunday Worship Leader" podcast

CHAPTER 2

The Worship Playbook

O ne of my favorite sports comedies of all time is *The Waterboy*, starring Adam Sandler. The movie follows a simpleminded Bobby Boucher as he goes from obscurity on the sidelines to leading the Mud Dogs to a college football championship. One of the main characters is his head coach, Coach Klein, who went from coaching at one of the most prestigious colleges in sports to the laughing stock of the state. How did he wind up there? He lost his playbook (well, it was actually stolen). Without his playbook he didn't know how to coach, and he was an anxious wreck until he realized his Cajun water boy was a secret weapon. Much like a coach utilizes his playbook to know which offense to call or how to penetrate a defense, worship leaders have a playbook that we can go to, a resource that spans back thousands of years, a world that church tradition and leaders have stepped into for generations.

Smack dab in the middle of the Bible, every worship leader has a playbook. It's comprised of 150 songs that I like to call "Israel's greatest hits." I can imagine the infomercial right now with David walking on a beach: "Have you ever wanted to cry out to God but don't have the right words to express your heart? Well, look no further. These 150 songs will take your worship life to the next level, with songs like 'The Lord Is My Shepherd' and 'Let Everything that Has Breath.' Call now, and don't delay!" The truth is, the book of Psalms is to a worship leader what a playbook would be for a football coach. It runs the gamut of human emotion, with everything from songs of triumph to laments of deep pain. Some of the most well-known songs we sing in churches worldwide, and songs that grace the radio, have lyrics hijacked straight from the Psalms. Hey, I'm guilty as well. One of my favorite worship songs that I've ever written comes straight out of Psalm 8: "O Lord, our Lord, how majestic is your name." I'm sure the psalmists are looking down and wondering where their royalty checks are.

While most people assume all of the Psalms were written by David (and, yes, he did write a lot), the truth is, they were written by a myriad of writers, including Ethan, Asaph, the sons of Korah, and Heman (no relation to the cartoon). Even the legendary Moses got in on the action. Solomon wrote two of them (Psalms 72 and 127). In fact, according to 1 Kings 4:32, Solomon wrote over a thousand songs. Like father, like son. Of course Solomon also gave us the only R-rated book in the Bible that most pastors still don't know what to do with. "Come next Sunday as we continue our series out of Song of Solomon, 'Turn out the lights.'"

But just as there is a diversity of writers of the psalms, so too there is a diversity of themes of the book. Some of the themes include psalms of confidence, thanksgiving, royalty (which address the spiritual role of a king in worshiping God), wisdom, and lament. Many modern worship songs grab ahold of themes like praise and thanksgiving, but you may be surprised to know that there are more psalms of lament than any other theme. The struggle with anxiety and depression has been around since the Old Testament times. I think we do a huge disservice when we leave these incredibly vulnerable and authentic songs of the human condition off the table. I love what some worship leaders and song-writers are doing today by restoring the idea of laments in our church context of worship. If we're honest, life can drag us down sometimes.

Psalm 51 is one of the most gut-wrenching songs, not just because of the lyrics, but because of the season of life that it was written in. David had just committed adultery with Bathsheba, had her husband killed to cover it all up, and as a consequence of his actions, the son that was born from the infidelity died after just a week of life (see 2 Sam. 12). This is a song of repentance and prayer. Perhaps the most poetic line from this song comes in verses 10 and 11: "Create in me a pure heart O God, and renew a steadfast spirit within me. Do not cast me from your presence or take your Holy Spirit from me." These two lines alone pack in so much theology that instantly we're reminded how valuable the book of Psalms is. David is asking God to give him a new heart, something that foreshadows the purpose of Jesus coming to earth. Centuries after David wrote this song Jesus would lay down His life so that we might be born again. "Therefore if anyone is in Christ, he is a new creation" (2 Cor. 5:17). David is asking God to allow him to stay in His presence. David knew that being in the presence of God is more valuable than anything else this world has to offer. Here he nods to the distinguishing presence that only comes to awareness in worship—the manifest presence of God. This type of presence is different from omnipresence, where God is everywhere all the time. David writes about the omnipresence of God in his famous Psalm 139:

> Where can I go from your Spirit?
>   Where can I flee from your presence?
> If I go up to the heavens, you are there;
>   if I make my bed in the depths, you are there.
> If I rise on the wings of the dawn,
>   if I settle on the far side of the sea,
> even there your hand will guide me,
>   your right hand will hold me fast

This manifest presence is the life-changing, almost tangible awareness that comes in the fullness of God's love. It's what David writes about in his famous Psalm 84, another psalm that Matt Redman adapted with "Better is One Day."

> How lovely is your dwelling place,
>   Lord Almighty!
> My soul yearns, even faints,
>   for the courts of the Lord;
> my heart and my flesh cry out
>   for the living God. (Ps. 84:1-2)

I've had moments in worship when I've sensed an undeniable nearness of God, when I can almost tangibly feel His embrace. This is the type of presence that David craved and never wanted to be banished from in Psalm 51. In his book *The Pursuit of God*, author and pastor A.

W. Tozer wrote, "The Presence and the manifestation of the Presence are not the same. There can be one without the other. God is here when we are wholly unaware of it. He is manifest only when and as we are aware of His Presence. On our part there must be surrender to the Spirit of God, for His work is to show us the Father and the Son."

Also in Psalm 51, we see the revelation that long before Pentecost happens in Acts 2, the Holy Spirit was active and at work in certain people throughout the Old Testament, David being one of those people. There's so much theology packed into just two verses of one psalm in a book of 150 of them. It's easy to see the value of knowing this book and keeping it close to heart.

More and more I'm hearing from worship leaders across the country that psalms of lament are finding their way back into worship services all across the globe in this day and age. Songwriters are also writing new worship songs of lament, which are connecting with the church through vulnerability and authenticity. Here's the truth: there are people in your church who are going through pain, loss, and hardship. If there's anything we've learned walking through these last couple of years, it's that people are hurting. There is an honest connection that can happen in worship when our songs reflect our journey. Yes, we know that the cross has the final word, and there is victory for those who are in Christ Jesus, but there is also the tension of living in the here and now, where trials are real and faith is tested. Jesus said it honestly in John 16:33: "In this world you will have trouble. But take heart! I have overcome the world."

One of my closest friends is Chris Douglas, the current worship pastor at National Community Church. In 2017 he and his wife, Kathryn, lost their baby girl Keelyn to a heart defect when she was barely six months old. There is no category for the type of pain that loss brings. Chris and Kathryn responded to this tragic season of hurt the only way they knew how—in worship. In the midst of their suffering they brought God their questions and their pain, but much like Job in the Old Testament, they never turned away from the Lord. Through this gut-wrenching trial, Chris picked up his guitar and for the first time in a long time began to sing a new song. The lyrics he penned were honest and undoubtedly hard for him to sing. But in his obedience and pursuit of God, his song has led to so many stories of healing and wholeness—proof that God will use our pain to bring His promise.

Here are a couple of lines from Chris's song "Fall into Kindness":

I fall into kindness
I cannot explain
In all of the waiting
In every prayer I've prayed
I fall into kindness
I'm choosing to trust
Here where You meet me
You're with me

God wants us to speak and sing to Him just as much during these moments of hardship as when we're living on cloud nine. In fact, I would argue that He wants to hear from us *more* in those seasons of pain and suffering. We need to sing the gamut of the Psalms in our churches—praises of joy, triumphant worship, heartfelt laments, and everything in between.

The Psalms can be an incredible guideline as you lead a worship service. As you journey through your song set, don't just think about keys and tempos, or which song has the sickest synth bass drop at the bridge. Think about lyrical content. Are we singing all songs of praise and no songs of lament? Do we intentionally open with a song of thanksgiving, or are we happy to just pop in any upbeat song to kick off a worship set? There are some beautiful lessons the book of Psalms can teach us as we approach how we pick a song set and what we are leading our church to sing. This is where the idea of a playbook really comes into play, and we almost get some instructional guidance in the ancient text. Remember that in the era these were written, there was no particular "worship leader" role in the context that we understand it today. The notion that there would be a band onstage with lights, ProPresenter casting lyrics on a screen, and a crowd of people following the lead of one person singing would be as foreign a concept as if we went back to the medieval times in skinny jeans and showed them an iPhone.

What we do know is that corporate worship existed in ancient Israel, and in David's reign in particular, he took it to another level by bringing in skilled musicians and establishing a ground level of excellence (see 1 Chron. 25). The Psalms are packed with applications to our modern-day worship experience. For example, Psalm 100:4 reads, "Enter His gates with thanksgiving and His courts with praise; give thanks to Him and praise His name." In this passage, there's the idea that our thanksgiving leads us into His presence. David would be familiar with the layout of the Tabernacle, where we see outer courts, inner courts, and finally the Holy of Holies. I find it helpful in referencing this as I choose songs for a Sunday morning. The outer courts would be our lobby, the inner courts our sanctuary, and the Holy of Holies the altar place. Or think of it as the first song grabbing everyone's attention, almost a call to worship. Then the next couple of songs take you a little deeper in theology and in spirit. Then the last song gets you to a place where the heart is a tilled field, ready for the seed to be planted.

Kicking off your worship service with an upbeat praise song makes sense, and it falls in line with Psalm 100. This isn't a special formula, and anything that becomes routine is exactly that—*routine*. Sometimes you may feel the need to open with something not so fast, or even with a Scripture reading. But however you open the worship service, fix it on Jesus, and start with praise!

When we come to God with a heart of gratitude, we enter His courts. Obviously the "entering" part is a beginning, the first step, almost the starting line. So, what if the first song you led in your worship service was intentionally a song of giving thanks, coming into His courts with grateful hearts?

Another great passage to reference in our 21st century worship experience is from Psalm 150. Here we get a rundown of the instruments that were used and how each instrument was designed to bring praise. We've got trumpets, harps, lyres, strings, pipes, and cymbals. I'm pretty sure people were even complaining back then how loud the music was. But David didn't care. He was charging his musicians to praise with what they had, from the depths of their hearts. The word "praise" means to ascribe worth. So by playing your instrument, you were telling God how worthy He is. It kind of puts things in a different perspective when you realize you're not just keeping a beat on the drums but also telling God how awesome He is by the way you play.

The breakdown: we need to get into the Psalms so that they can get into us. Read them, know them, study them, even memorize some of them. (Maybe you could memorize Psalm 117, the shortest chapter in the Bible. If you want to hit over-achiever status, try Psalm 119, the longest chapter in the Bible.) As you study, you'll realize that so many songs that you lead every weekend are tied into these ancient ballads. Read from the Psalms and connect the Scripture to the song for your congregation. For instance, the next time you lead Matt Redman's "10,000 Reasons," you could tie it to Psalm 103 and mention how David wrote these words most likely later in his life as he looked back on the many blessings God had given him. Or try opening your service with a call to worship from Psalm 96:

> Sing to the Lord a new song;
> > sing to the Lord, all the earth.
> Sing to the Lord, praise His name;
> > proclaim His salvation day after day.
> Declare His glory among the nations,
> > His marvelous deeds among all peoples.

The Psalms are such a timeless piece of Scripture to us because these songs don't just appear in the middle of the Bible; they make cameos throughout the Bible. The Psalms are quoted throughout the Bible in different moments. The New Testament has nearly 75 references to the Psalms, and Paul quotes the psalms 14 different times in his letter to the Romans. Jesus knew them well. In fact, during His post-resurrection breakfast with the disciples, He told them that everything that had happened to Him was to fulfill the Law of Moses, the Prophets, and the Psalms (see Luke 24:44). Clearly the book of Psalms is central to God's working throughout Scripture. And it's filled with instruction and lessons that we can lean into for life. When you put a melody to a message, it gets into your memory. Singing is proven to be one of the best ways to learn. Right from the beginning of the book of Psalms we get this point. Psalm 1 kicks off:

> Blessed is the one who does not walk in step with the wicked or stand in the way that sinners take or sit in the company of mockers, but whose delight is in the law of the Lord, and who meditates on His law day and night.

We quickly learn that whoever writes the songs is someone who meditates on the Word of God day and night. What does "meditate" mean? To focus on. Many meditation practices have music involved to bring peace into the atmosphere. I'm not talking Eastern religion here, or anything hocus pocus. I'm saying that meditation is tied into the Psalms, and even into the *selah* moments we see scattered throughout the book.

In our weekend services as we lead worship, we should be taking people on a journey. For a journey to be true, it must include the twists and turns of life, not just the smooth, straight paths. You can't have all mountains and no valleys. Likewise, you can have all valleys and no mountains. Psalms is a well-rounded expression of a life in worship. It's an incredible memoir of songs written by many Israelites all coming from different experiences. We have to remember that when we lead worship in our churches there are people with different experiences that they bring in. You could all be singing the same song but because of the different journeys people are on they may all have a different song that comes from their heart. For instance when singing the hymn "Great Is Thy Faithfulness," the images of my life where God has been faithful probably look a lot different from yours.

You want to lead songs that speak to a multitude of experiences. To be a well-rounded worship leader, it's not just about having fast, slow, and medium songs; the content of those songs has to be a broad picture of who God is. A. W. Tozer said that the most important thing about you is what pops into your mind when you think about God. As worship leaders we get to help people shape their theology of a loving God who works in every season of life. I like to say that one of our jobs is to put a magnifying glass on the character of God. The Psalms express all of these human experiences and godly characteristics in a beautiful, sometimes tragic, and uplifting way.

Another practical takeaway from knowing the Psalms is in training your team and raising up leaders. There are guidelines for musicianship and leadership in the psalms. For instance, Psalm 33:3 says, "Sing to Him a new song; play skillfully, and shout for joy." In that one verse we get the mandate to write new songs and to play with excellence—two things that every worship team can benefit from. One of my favorite leadership quotes comes from Psalm 78:72 which says, "And David shepherded them with integrity of heart; with skillful hands he led them." Asaph, the writer of this particular song, is reminding us that David was such a powerful leader and inspiring king because he had character *and* skill. It takes both to be a leader in the Church.

What if you opened your rehearsals simply by sharing a psalm with your team. We can use the Psalms to rally the troops and inspire our teams with the why behind the what. You can inspire your team to unity with Psalm 133. Or you can inspire them to play wholeheartedly with Psalm 150. The more you dive into the psalms as a team, the stronger your team will be.

The spiritual strength of knowing the Psalms is that, like a good workout, it builds your worship muscle. If you're not feeding your spirit, then you're starving it. And I can't think of a better four-course meal than the book of Psalms. Try reading a psalm a day over the next 150 days. Start your mornings off with the ancient lyrics that have shaped worship cultures for thousands of years. Don't just read through a psalm to get your check mark on Bible reading for the day. Read it, and like David wrote in Psalm 119, meditate on it. Let the message, context, and overall feel pierce your heart. Let God speak through these songs. Let Him sing over you! We know God sings over us according to Zephaniah 3:17.

Maybe you need to read a chapter in a quiet place and just take 10 minutes to let the Spirit of God minister to you. Then try picking up a guitar, sitting at the piano, or using your voice to just sing the psalm that you read. Put a new melody to it—not to get your songwriting credit, but just to sing to the Lord. These psalms are offense, marching into enemy territory. And they're defense against the attack of the enemy. A coach is not much of a coach without his playbook to go to. And I would say worship leaders aren't much without the book of Psalms. It's not a manual but it is a reference. So get into the Psalms, and let them get into you!

Closing Thought

Hey y'all, this is Paul Wilbur. I have been leading worship and writing from the book of Psalms ever since I surrendered my life to Yeshua (Jesus) way back in March 1977. Back then, Keith Green was one of my musical heroes, along with Second Chapter of Acts and a family ministry called The Archers. As a young Jewish guy singing in the choir at Temple, the Psalms were a consistent source of material for the liturgy; and even though we sang them in Hebrew, they still carried a special presence about them.

For my heart, the difference in the psalms, indeed in worship itself, is in the pronouns. For instance, the word most translated "worship" in the Bible is the Hebrew word *shachah* (pronounced "shah-chah"). It means to bow low, even to prostrate oneself. If you think about the physical position of the Muslim at prayer, this would be a more accurate demonstration of *shachah* than to stand upright with our hands lifted up to the heavens. And consider who we have come to worship in the sanctuary. Many of our modern choruses that we call "worship songs" find us speaking to each other about God rather than speaking directly to Him.

I am not getting critical here. I'm simply trying to steer our love boat in the right direction. The Greek word for worship is *proskuneo*, meaning "to kiss toward" or "to kiss the hand." There is a humility of posture and attitude that is demonstrated in each of these languages. Have you ever seen an Orthodox Jewish man praying at the Western Wall in Jerusalem? His knees are bent, he is hunched over, and he sways forward and backward. It is an attitude of weakness and submission with his eyes closed so that he is not distracted by all the motion and commotion around him. And so it is in the Psalms; the verses are directed toward the One who is the object of the psalmist's affection. The Psalms, in my opinion, are the best source of intimate expressions of love, adoration, and worship that can be found in all of Scripture. And that is why, when it is worship that I am after, you will find me selah-ing in the Psalms.

Paul Wilbur
Artist-in-residence and apostolic team member, Celebration Church, Jacksonville, FL

CHAPTER 3

Pastoring Through Worship

I 'll never forget Thanksgiving Day 1996. I was 14 years old, and my brother, cousin, and I were outside shooting basketball when I had the bright idea to dunk the basketball by jumping off a two-foot platform. I was barely five feet tall at this point, so I needed a little help if I was going to do my best Michael Jordan dunk. I managed to make a pretty spectacular slam, if I do say so myself, but the landing was even more spectacular. Breaking my tibia and fibula bones upon impact, it made for a pretty awful Turkey Day. I spent the next 10 weeks in a cast watching nothing but college basketball and the NBA. I've still got the scar, two screws, and metal plate in my leg to remind me!

My hoop dreams as a young teenager could only be lived out vicariously through my favorite players. During those months, my obsession with basketball went to a whole new level. My room was already flooded with posters of Michael Jordan and Shaq, and I had thousands of trading cards scattered across my bedroom floor. Yet in these laid-up months on a couch, I began to study the game, understanding how each position played a key role in making up the team. You truly need all five positions to make up a well-rounded team: center, power forward, small forward, shooting guard, and point guard. You can't have a team made up of all point guards. They might be fast and great passers, but going up against the height of a center, they stand no chance in the lane. On the flip side, a team made up of all seven-footers would be incredible at blocking and rebounding but they might lack the speed and agility it takes to get up and down the court in time.

Most of history's greatest teams, like the unstoppable Chicago Bulls of the '90s, were made of incredible players at all five positions. The dynamic duos throughout professional basketball understood their roles and didn't try to get in each other's lane. Take Karl Malone and John Stockton of the Utah Jazz. Karl Malone, 14-time NBA All Star, played power forward and was one of the game's greatest rebounding-scoring threats. John Stockton, Malone's much shorter teammate, played point guard and to this day holds the record for most steals of all time and most assists in an NBA season. Malone didn't try to go for the assist record, and Stockton wasn't trying to dunk in the lane. They knew their roles and excelled at them.

Much like basketball has a five-lane highway to finding one's stride, the ministry within the church has a likewise model. Paul calls it the fivefold ministry:

> And He gave some as apostles, and some as prophets, and some as evangelists, and some as pastors and teachers, for the equipping of the saints for the work of service, to the building up of the body of Christ. (Eph. 4:11-12)

Right off the bat, I recognize that the title "worship leader" isn't one of those, but there's a tie-in for each of these areas when it comes to leading worship. I will also say that this is one of those areas in Scripture that has a lot of mystery and misunderstanding attached to it. Some church cultures exploit and abuse these titles and use them in an authoritarian way to push a position. That's not the Jesus way. Other churches don't even want to use the words in this passage for fear of getting it wrong, or they worry about others' perceptions. That's not the Jesus way either. As with anything in the kingdom of God, there is a balance, a harmony, and of course a mystery. I love mystery, because if we knew everything there was to know about everything, we wouldn't need to rely on the Holy Spirit. But we don't know everything, and He does. So I say this with one caveat: go to the Word of God and filter it for yourself. If anything in this book doesn't resonate with you, first have it pass through the filter of Scripture. What I say next I believe can help you identify a side of your heart and leadership that you may not have recognized before. So let's look at these five roles and how I believe they relate to leading worship within the Church.

The Apostle

"After this the Lord appointed seventy-two others and sent them two by two ahead of him to every town and place where he was about to go. He told them, 'The harvest is plentiful, but the workers are few. Ask the Lord of the harvest, therefore, to send out workers into His harvest field'" (Luke 10:1-2).

The same Luke who wrote this Gospel also wrote another book, called Acts. The full name is Acts of the Apostles. It's a written record of the stuff the sent ones did. And they did some wild stuff. The word "apostle" translates to "sent one."

At the time of Paul and Luke, Rome was conquering lands and taking over the world. And everywhere they conquered, they wanted that land to *become* Rome. They wanted their rules, philosophies, art, and ways of life to basically take over the earth. So the Roman emperor sent out people known as "apostles" to establish Roman culture wherever they went. The Gospel takes the term and flips it around to be about the Kingdom. Jesus sent out His apostles to take the Kingdom life wherever they went. It was a new culture, a new way of thinking—bringing the gospel, and the full life mentioned in John 10:10, to a world in need of something different.

In the Bible, the title "apostle" is attached to those who were sent on mission and brought the kingdom of heaven to Earth. Paul, who wrote half of the New Testament, planted at least 14 churches, and wrote this particular passage, was considered an apostle. Jesus' disciples, after the Day of Pentecost, are referred to as apostles. In a sense, they go from being students to teachers. They were establishing the early church. They were bringing the culture of the Kingdom to their day and age. There is a nuance of a fathering spirit in an apostle. They are culture-setters, leaders, and planters, and they are passionate about raising up others into their full potential.

In the worship-leading realm, I think of someone who is raising other leaders. Although these friends would never expect or look for this title, I have a few examples of worship pastors and leaders who have an apostolic mantle on them. I look at Aaron Keyes, who started the 10,000 Fathers School of Worship and has had moments of pouring into me and the other worship leaders at National Community Church during my time there. I think of Bob Kauflin, who has been faithfully leading within the Sovereign Grace movement for decades, raising hundreds of worship leaders, and pastoring thousands more through his books. If you are someone who's been given charge to set culture and raise other leaders, you may already be running in this lane.

The Prophet

Worship is prophetic in that it declares the goodness of God over our situations and leads people to focus on Christ. Here's how my NIV Study Bible describes the role of a prophet: people to whom God made known a message for His people that was appropriate to their particular need or situation. If worship leading doesn't lean into that, I don't know what does. Prophecy and the role of a prophet can definitely be taken out of context, and out of the five roles in this Ephesians passage, the prophet role probably draws the most controversy. However many different denominations, church traditions, and upbringings exist, there are probably that many different viewpoints on the prophetic! Here's a baseline that we can go to for what this role does: *"But one who prophesies strengthens others, encourages them, and comforts them" (1 Cor. 14:3).*

I have been in some environments where the prophetic goes from mysterious to downright weird. Weird turns people off, and sadly that can repel hearts from the gospel. Jesus wasn't weird. In fact, He drew thousands of people to Him because He had a quality that was attractive, not repellent. Jesus spoke life over people, strengthened them, and brought encouragement and comfort. He was a prophet. I believe we have many worship leaders and songwriters in our midst who operate in the prophetic in a way that makes Jesus smile. They sing songs of life and encouragement over their congregations. They bring melodies of comfort and strength. If you're writing songs that contain a message from God for your people, you could be running in this lane.

Music and the prophetic often go hand in hand. In 1 Samuel 16, David was called on to play his lyre for Saul to bring Saul comfort when he was tormented by the "evil spirit from God." I wish we had time to go into *that* one—or maybe I don't. Regardless, David brought a prophetic type of comfort through the ministry of music.

In 2 Kings 3, the prophet Elisha asked specifically for a harpist so that God would speak to him: "'But now bring me a harpist.' While the harpist was playing, the hand of the Lord came on Elisha and he said, 'This is what the Lord says: I will fill this valley with pools of water'" (2 Kings 3:15-16). When the music played, the prophetic message came.

I've said it before that music is a message, and when you put the words of God to the melody of worship, I believe the Spirit travels on sound. When I think of worship leaders living in this lane, Leeland comes to mind. In his live album *Better Word*, there are times when he just sings off script over the moment and over the people in attendance. Jesus Culture, Bethel Music, and many other movements carry this calling in a special way.

The Evangelist

Thanks to some really bad television, this role has gotten some negativity attached to it. There are definitely phonies out there, but there are also undeniably gifted evangelists who simply have the ability to present the gospel and draw people in with the message of Christ. Evangelists help people through their testimony. In the Greek language, the word *euangelistas* means "bearer of good tidings." I don't know about you, but I like that name! Songs can be testimonies put to music. Songs can lead people back to their Maker. Like the legend of the Pied Piper playing a song that drew the rats out of the town (sorry for that analogy), a melody can catch our ears and take us to a place where our hearts are receptive. A song can break down walls and open up hearts to the gospel. Music cuts straight to the heart without ever asking for permission.

I would say Hillsong Worship has a very evangelistic heart in that they always give a call to salvation in their concerts and they are incredibly missional their approach to ministry. The songs they write and release are about the goodness of God and the love of Christ. Songs like "Who You Say I Am" speak to the identity we have when we make Jesus our Lord. I've had the opportunity to sit in a room with some of their leaders and hear firsthand the goal of their ministry: leading people to find salvation in Jesus. They not only release albums through different age-targeted ministries but also movies, books, and other forms of art. They are one of the biggest Christian influences on culture at large.

If you can't stop talking about the love of Jesus, sharing the power of the cross, and singing of the resurrection life that is offered to anyone who would call on His name, then you may be a worship leader with an evangelistic heart.

The Pastor

This is probably the most obvious of the five when it comes to leading worship. The original term means shepherd, as in one who watches over, protects, and guides a flock. When I was growing up, people always called a congregation a flock, but I guess that's not as common in our language today. Aaron Keyes once said, "Worship pastors lead people, and worship leaders lead songs. We don't need any more worship leaders." I think he's got a point. We need more people who care about people.

A pastor has a heart for the Church, to see people discover who Jesus is and be transformed by the power of His love. "Pastoral care" is a term being used more and more in ministry, and there's a giant need for it today. A pastor is more concerned with authenticity and transformation than becoming the next big name on the radio charts. A pastor knows the name of church members and not just team members. A pastor calls up his drummer when they just lost their day job instead of just texting them when they need a fill-in. True pastors care more about making disciples than gaining a social media following. If your heart breaks for the things that break the heart of God, you might be living with a pastoral burden. Jesus had many titles, but one of my favorites is the "Good Shepherd." I imagine He was called the good one because there may have been quite a few bad ones. Jesus is the pastor's pastor. He sets the bar for what a pastor should aspire to be.

A quick example in our worship context of a pastor is Chris Tomlin. I've been in the room when he's led worship, and there's a sense of trust and care in the atmosphere. You trust that he's been where he's about to take everyone. When he leads worship, you feel like you are being taken care of, like you're being shepherded in worship. There's a relational element to leading worship, and people want to trust that you're taking them in the right direction, toward the heart of God. Worship leaders shepherd people and shepherd moments. You have to be in tune to how the Spirit is moving to know how to shepherd a moment. There could be something that God wants to connect His children to in a song or a lyric. So that might look like vamping a section of the song and repeating a particular line so that people can grab ahold of it. There could be a verse of Scripture that ties together two songs in a powerful way. This is where the teaching role connects to pastoring. Or maybe God has been pressing on your heart to share a piece of your testimony as it relates to a song. Your testimony could bring freedom to someone in your congregation.

To know how to pastor well, you have to look at what it takes to shepherd. The Old Testament is full of examples of shepherds; Abraham, Moses, Jacob, and David are just a handful. Rachel was a shepherdess. For the example of worship, we'll go with David and highlight the way that he shepherded. According to Psalm 78:72, "David shepherded them with integrity of heart; with skillful hands he led them." It takes integrity and skill to properly pastor people. David was a skilled warrior, poet, leader, and shepherd. But it wasn't his skill that kept him on the throne as the greatest king Israel ever had. It was his integrity. He did things *for* the people instead of living to get things *from* the people. He wanted the nation to prosper and be at peace.

It takes both skill and heart, not one or the other, to be a worship pastor. If you have all the ability to write songs, can rip up the guitar, and have a voice that melts butter, but you have no character, your leadership won't have a lasting impact. On the flip side, you could be the most reliable and trustworthy worship leader in the world, but if you don't know how to read a chord chart, or play in time, or carry a tune, you probably won't have the respect or platform to pour into a team. Shepherding takes heart and skill. Begin to think about your role not just as a leader of songs but as a shepherd of people and moments. I am inspired by the way William McDowell leads worship. He is a shepherd in worship, and if you've ever heard or seen him in that environment, you know that there is a shifting of the atmosphere from the anointing he carries so gracefully. We need more worship pastors.

The Teacher

Think of your favorite teacher growing up. Mine was Mrs. Arnold in second grade. She was the epitome of gentleness. In college my favorite professor was Dr. Chris Neck. He's still a friend to this day, and his wisdom has challenged the way I think and operate. Just like in the education world, in the church world there are incredible teachers, gifted to help people gain access and application to the Word of God. Andy Stanley, Mark Batterson, T. D. Jakes, and Joyce Meyer are some incredible teachers who have been instrumental teachers in my life.

The words and ways of Jesus need to be taught, which is why the Great Commission has a teaching element to it in Matthew 28:20. There's an entire chapter later in this book dedicated to teaching through worship, so I won't overstate the need for this role, but it is vital to the health and life of the Church. Pastors and teachers are mentioned together in Ephesians 4 because their roles are closely related and they often work in tandem. There's a teaching requirement to pastoring, and there's a pastoring element involved in teaching. As my dad would often tell me, the Kingdom is more caught than taught. You teach just as much by your life as you do by your words. I recently heard John Mark Comer in a podcast say that we're called to live a life of example and invitation! Let your life be lived out in worship, teaching people what it looks like to be a fully devoted follower of Jesus. Let your words and your songs be used as instructions, providing a pathway to praise for your congregation.

A teacher in worship would potentially spend some time diving into the posture of praise, as we see in the psalms—teaching why we lift our hands, why we sing, kneel, bow, and other ways that we physically yield in humility and worship. Teachers help unmask the truth behind not only the methods of worship but also the depth of lyrics, living out John 4:23—spirit and truth. Lyrics are a lesson. Worship teaches theology, whether you're aware of that or not. So make sure you're teaching good theology! If there's a lyric that you think people might wrestle with, maybe unpack that a little. If there's a line that simply gets confusing, shine some light on it.

With an old hymn, you may want to explain the meaning of a word. In "Come Thou Fount," we see the phrase "like a fetter, bind my wandering heart to thee." I'm not sure the last time I heard "fetter" thrown out in a conversation, so that one might need some explanation. (It means "chain, or restraint" by the way.) Or how about the word "bulwark" in "A Mighty Fortress Is Our God"? Let's bring that one back! Anything that needs explanation is an opportunity to teach. Share a devotional with your team before rehearsal or on a Sunday right after service. Dive into the Scriptures with a small group and daily on your own. Teachers are learners first, so never stop learning! When you take seriously Colossians 3:16, you could be a worship teacher.

Tim Hughes and the Worship Central crew would definitely fall into this category. Whenever I get around him, I feel stretched and I want to just sit under his leadership. The Worship Central course that they've developed is one of the best resources for teams out there! And it's all free! The church Tim comes from, Holy Trinity Brompton, is a resource house. They founded Alpha, the Prayer Course, and many other teachings that have developed leaders throughout the global church. There's also something heavenly about hearing Nicky Gumbel's voice preaching. We need more godly teachers!

Growing in Your Gifting

I believe that of these five assignments, if you are leading worship or overseeing an aspect of ministry, the pastor role specifically is something that you need to keep close to heart.

I hope through these pages you have found a lane you identify with —not to restrict you, but to free you up. When you know which area you are gifted in, it shows you where you might need some support. A team that has all five of these areas represented somewhere in their heart is an unstoppable force. I don't just want a bunch of teachers on my worship team; I also need pastors and prophets. And so do you!

We need apostolic worship leaders in the world to raise up this generation and the next. We need evangelistic worship leaders writing and leading songs that introduce people to the hope of Jesus.

God operates with order and structure, so let's be mature in how we move in our gifting, but let's also be bold. If you don't already have a mentor, I pray this chapter has inspired you to find one. If you recognize a certain calling on the way you lead worship, find someone who operates in that gift who's a little further down the road than you are.

Remember that these roles are not to be misused or used as a crutch. In Ephesians 4:11, the way it starts might be the biggest takeaway you have from this entire chapter: "it was He who gave some…" It's Jesus who gives the gifts and assigns the roles, so we should never prop ourselves up or use a calling for personal gain or motivation. Never stop learning; never stop growing—and that includes growing in your gifting.

Closing Thought

It is incredible that there is not one verse in the entire New Testament that describes a worship leader. There is so much about worship and so much more about leadership, but absolutely nothing about (what we would identify as) worship leadership.

Leading people in worship should be like leading people in general; you will all have your style, your grace, your giftedness, your brokenness, and your blind spots. But if you can be aware of these, you will feel great release from the vague, all-encompassing pressure you once felt in pursuit of being all things to all people. Problems arise when certain gifts take prominence in any day and age, and suddenly everyone wants to lead like that superstar, most often to poor effect.

We need you leading like God has wired you to lead. If that's through apostolic, prophetic, pastoral means, then go for it! If God has wired you more to lead evangelistic methods, or didactic, go for it! We need each of these five graces operating in harmony so that the body of Christ may be built up in both unity and maturity (see Eph. 4). Like multiple lenses in a telescope, we need each of these graces working together in right relation to bring real clarity.

It takes all five. And it takes godly, grounded, mature leadership expressed in all five.

Godly, mature leaders will never be threatened or envious of other leaders gifted in other ways. (Think about Moses celebrating the gifting of Bezalel in Exodus 35:30-35.) Immature leaders will become insecure, petty, contentious. I know, because I've been all of those and worse. But when I remember and recognize what God has called me to be, I can then release what God has not called me to be, and I can rejoice in how God has raised up and spotlighted other leaders who have a grace other than my own.

Immaturity in a leader also leads one to ignore or minimize the various giftings in other leaders. If all you are is a hammer, the whole world becomes a nail. Sometimes you need a hammer and a nail; other times you need a sander or a screwdriver. Maturity recognizes the indispensable and interconnectedness of each of these roles.

Jesus fleshed out each of these five graces unlike anyone else ever has. Go through the Gospels with a watchful eye and you'll see Him elegantly operating in whatever grace was needed at the time. This is what maturity looks like: being supernaturally natural in the ways God has graced you to lead, and being both intentional and developmental in the ways you're undernourished.

You do not need to be proficient in each of these, but that does not absolve you, or any of us for that matter, of the need to continually strive to grow up into the fullness of Christ.

Aaron Keyes
Worship pastor; founder, 10,000 Fathers School of Worship

CHAPTER 4

You've Got to Pray

When I was in second grade, MC Hammer was all the rage. All my classmates wore parachute pants to school, and my friends and I did the "hammer time" dance as best we could anytime recess was in session. My dance moves haven't really evolved much over time, but that's just not my spiritual gift. One of Hammer's biggest hits, "Pray," had a pretty simple message. It's in the title of this chapter, if you didn't put that together yet. Simple but true. I often wonder how many worship leaders get onstage every Sunday to lead their churches in corporate worship and then go home to a bland or, worse, nonexistent prayer life. I believe the consistency of your private prayer life will determine the power and authenticity of your public worship life. You can't know the Father if you never talk to Him. And that's what prayer is in its simplest definition: having a conversation with God.

If you haven't heard His voice speak lately, I would ask, when was the last time He heard *yours*? As you comb through the Bible, you can see a pattern: those who know God the most are the ones who spend the most time with Him. Abraham prayed all the time. In fact, he was so comfortable in his conversations with God that he negotiated with Him in one of the boldest prayers ever as he pleaded for the cities of Sodom and Gomorrah in Genesis 18. Moses talked to God on the regular. David prayed so much that he wrote songs out of his prayers. I've said it before, worship songs are prayers put to melody. Whenever you see someone being used mightily by God in Scripture, look at their prayer life. There's always a passionate consistency.

Jesus, the Prayer Jedi

It comes as no surprise that Jesus tops everyone in His prayer life. Scripture tells us Jesus got up early in the morning to pray (see Mark 1:35), and He often withdrew to get alone with God (see Luke 5:16). These are two patterns that I try to copy and paste into my daily rhythms. In the summer of 2019 we dropped some coinage to get my dream back deck built. Tin roof, vintage lights, nice view of the woods. During the height of the pandemic our family spent entire days on the back deck. It's my special place. I've developed a routine in the mornings fashioned after Jesus' prayer habits. After I kiss the kids off to school, I head out to the deck to pray, with my cup of Folgers coffee in hand (I know all you coffee snobs just fell back in your chairs, but don't lose focus). It's usually about half an hour of prayer, or by the time my first cup of coffee is gone. Sometimes I do a lot of talking, but most times I'm still and quiet in His presence, tuning in to the still small voice of the Holy Spirit.

When I was in youth group, or at Christian summer camp, we called these moments "quiet time." It's not as much in our language these days, but maybe we should bring it back in style!

Do you have a quiet time? Everything in our world is loud, with a thousand voices distracting you and pulling you away from the quiet place. That's why as leaders (and more importantly as Christ-followers), we have to be intentional about creating this sacred space, getting alone with the Father. I would encourage you to carve out time every day to start your mornings off right. You will notice a difference. You'll see a greater peace flood your days. You'll feel a sense of joy in the small things. You'll develop a greater love for your team, your friends, your family, and your church. You'll be more effective in your work and you may even start to feel like you're striving less. I'm challenged by Martin Luther, the great reformation leader, who once said, "I have so much to do today that I'm going to need to spend three hours in prayer in order to be able to get it all done."

There's an ancient idea through the centuries of the Church called the "daily office"—dating back to a book called *The Rule of St. Benedict* in AD 516. This particular monk had divided the day into eight different prayer segments, a monastic timetable, so that they could stay in a constant state of prayer. St. Benedict, along with many monks throughout the ages, probably got his inspiration from David: "Seven times a day I praise you for your righteous laws" (Ps. 119:164).

Before you set about your day with all the tasks, meetings, and plans that have to get done, cover it in prayer. Bring your day-planner to Jesus and ask Him for guidance through His Spirit. If I'm honest with you, my most common prayer is simple: "Help me." I need help, and God knows that; He just wants me to ask for it. When His blessing is on your day, you can't lose! I love to connect with worship leadership online, so recently I did a 10-week online course called "Worship Camp Online." In our first ever WCO session, I asked worship leaders to submit questions and topics they were currently wrestling with. The very first question that came in was "What do you consider to be the best prayers to pray over your team?" I love the heart behind this question, and it launched into one of my favorite talks ever. I've spent the beginning of this chapter stating the importance of having a prayer life. It's everything. Now, in the remainder of this chapter, I want to dive into some specific ways we can pray *for* and *with* our team, what to pray, and how to pray, as we look deeper into the greatest team ever assembled. No, not the Avengers. I'm talking Jesus and the 12 disciples.

Prayer Leads to Influence

A leader can only lead to *the level of influence that he has with his followers.* Think about the 12 disciples for a moment. Every single one of them, besides John and Judas, became a martyr and died for the cause of the Church. Ten sane, confident men don't do that for someone unless that person has tremendous influence in their lives. Clearly, Jesus had built that influence over a short span of three years as He walked, ate, slept, and did life with His team. And something we can't afford to miss? He prayed for them. When it comes to our context of leading worship teams, you can't pastor people if you're not praying for them.

Make sure you are intentionally and regularly praying for your team. Ask them for prayer requests, in person or over email. During my time as worship director at National Community Church, we launched a Facebook page where team members could share prayer requests and praise reports, and our entire team across eight campuses would join in agreement and prayer over those requests. Sometimes they were super-heavy battles like cancer or losing a loved one. Other times people shared about job interviews or troubles with relationships. Whatever the case, there was a space for the team to share their need for prayer. I'd encourage you to create a space for that.

It could be as simple as opening and closing your rehearsal times with prayer. I've done this with nearly every team I've had the opportunity to lead, as it builds trust and community. When you're praying for your team, and the team is praying for you, there's a deeper connection that goes far beyond Sunday mornings. Love is forged. I love it when someone from the team emails me on a Friday about a prayer request I shared on Wednesday. It shows me that they're thinking about my situation and they care for me. This is a two-way street. In a culture where it's so easy to feel overlooked and forgotten, how much value does a simple text or phone call bestow? Don't rush right into practicing songs and miss the chance to be of service and pray for your team. Turn a rehearsal into a prayer meeting. It doesn't have to go for an hour, but give people the chance and space to pray, and cultivate it into your team.

Unity and Healing

Prayer also has the power to heal. Broken relationships can be restored on the other side of prayer. Maybe you've had an experience where you had serious tension and conflict with someone on your team or staff. No, just me? Okay, cool. Let me get real here. Relationships are messy. Community is hard. When you lead worship with a team, the enemy *hates* unity, and he will do whatever he can to bring division. That often occurs in the world of relationships.

There was a season a few years ago when I was constantly walking on eggshells with a certain worship leader on my team. I don't know what I said or did, but everything seemed to be taken out of context and was received as an attack. I couldn't win! So I started praying for them. "God, will you change this person's heart? Make them see my side and how I'm right." Okay, it wasn't exactly like that, but I did ask God to change them. And guess what God showed me? He revealed that I was the one who needed to change. Instead of praying that God would shift their perspective, I prayed that He would grow mine. And as I prayed daily for this person, the Holy Spirit began to do what He does so well: bring unity. The tension slowly disappeared, and the bonds of trust were mended. I'm happy to say that my friendship with this leader is great today, but I wonder if I had let my pride get the best of me. You see, pride is the biggest obstacle to a culture of prayer. We think we don't *need* to pray for a person, a team, or a move. We got this! Or we have too much to do to pray. We let prayer become a last resort when it needs to be our first response!

Pray Together, Stay Together

When it comes to our team that God has entrusted to us, often we can forget to pray for those closest to us! You've heard the saying, "familiarity breeds contempt." Don't let that happen in your life! I have found that praying for someone automatically turns to loving them in a greater capacity. Isn't it wild to think that when Jesus prayed for His disciples, when He washed their feet, when He did life with them, He did so including Judas, knowing that his betrayal was around the corner? Jesus never stopped loving Judas, and He prayed for him along with the others.

I've talked about praying *for* your team, but it's also key to pray as a team, especially if you have a staff that meets regularly. Don't get so swamped in meetings and planning that you don't pray together. Pray for your church, for your city, and for the community God is growing. Pray for each other with each other. Seek the Lord's face together. Find ways to do this outside of rehearsals and service times.

One of the best things I've implemented as a worship pastor is "Creative Fridays." Every week, Friday is our day to write, record, shoot a video, or do something that stretches our creativity. But the way we start Fridays is even better. We spend an hour, as a team, in prayer and devotion. More times than not, it is actually a prayer or a scripture that someone shares in this time that inspires the song or recording that follows. Sometimes we continue our prayer time in breakthrough intercession. Prayer will yield a greater level of creativity on your team! After all, one idea from the Holy Spirit is better than anything you could come up with in your own strength. So pray for songs, downloads from heaven. Ask God to show you what your church needs to be singing. What are the songs you should be writing? Every worship song starts as a prayer. I would encourage you to journal as you pray, and have your team journal as well. Write down those prayers that you are praying for your church, and watch as some of them become songs that your church will sing!

Teach Us to Pray

As I said earlier, Jesus gives us the golden standard on how to cultivate a healthy prayer life. He gave His followers prayer lessons often. When they could have asked Jesus to teach them anything, they asked how to pray (see Luke 11)! I probably would have asked how to do that water-walking trick. How cool of a selfie would that be?

Jesus taught them what we call "The Lord's Prayer" in that chapter. It's one of the most powerful prayers in Scripture. One of my other favorite prayers by Jesus happens just before His trial, crucifixion, death, and resurrection. In John 17, Jesus prays first for Himself, then for His followers, and finally for all believers, then and now. This is huge. Don't forget to pray for yourself! I think once you pray for yourself, you'll know what to pray for others. It's not a selfish way to pray; it's something Jesus demonstrated. I have to pray for myself, because I *need* God in my life more than I need myself. Jesus prayed for Himself, but it wasn't *about* Him; it was about glorifying the Father and leading people to know the Father. Everything Jesus did pointed to His Father.

After He prayed over Himself, Christ prayed for His disciples: "I pray for them. I am not praying for the world, but for those you have given me, for they are yours" (John 17:9).

I love the words "those you have given me." Think about who God has given you. Perhaps your worship team would fall into that category. How are you stewarding those He has entrusted under your leadership? Praying for them is a way to honor that position.

He prays specifically for their oneness (v. 11), their joy (v. 13), their protection (v. 15), and their sanctification (v. 17)—all subject matter that we can pray over our teams in this day and age. But there is one particular point from John 17 that I want to highlight that you can pray over your team specifically.

As Jesus launches into the next phase of His prayer, we read His prayer for not only those who believed back then but also for those who would believe later on. That's you and me. Here's what He prayed:

> My prayer is not for them alone. I pray also for those who will believe in me through their message, that all of them may be one, Father, just as you are in me and I am in you. May they also be in us so that the world may believe that you have sent me. I have given them the glory that you gave me, that they may be

one as we are one—I in them and you in me—so that they may be brought to complete unity. Then the world will know that you sent me and have loved them even as you have loved me. (John 17:20-23)

There's a lot of "one" in that prayer, and that's what we need today more than ever before. In a world that is divided, with people fighting in politics, social media threads, and sadly across denominational lines, complete unity is what Christ prayed for His Church.

On your team, unity and community lead to chemistry, which leads to flowing with one another in anointing. I like to say community offstage leads to chemistry onstage. Chemistry is the special sauce in a band's sound. One of my favorite bands from the '90s, Oasis, always struggled with this. They had essentially two lead singers, brothers Liam and Noel Gallagher. They wrote some amazing songs and had an incredible live show, when they weren't fighting. And that was the band's ultimate demise. They broke up over an argument that almost went to court. And they were family!

Sadly, on a worship team there can exist division over silly feuds as well. People can focus on the small things and lose the unity. Pray for that, and pray for it hard.

Thank You, Jesus

Another mindset to have in praying for your team is thanksgiving. Jesus constantly gave thanks in His prayers, many times proceeding a miracle, such as feeding the 5,000 in Matthew 14 and before raising Lazarus to life in John 11. First Thessalonians 5:18 tells us to "give thanks in all circumstances." Do you ever just thank God for who you have on your team? Thank God for who you have in your ministry instead of focusing on who you don't have or on what positions you need. They will come in time. Thank God for your pastors and production team. Remember, without a production team you won't make much of an impact. You can have the greatest band in the world, but without a person to mix them, it's not going to have a sound.

Thank God for the opportunities He's given you, for the gifts He's bestowed on you. Thank Him for calling, for purpose, for the cross, for a hope and future. The list could go on and on. Before coming to God with your list of wants and needs, open your prayers with a list of gratitude for all the blessings in your life. You will begin to see more of what God has already done in your life! Keep a prayer journal, and come up with new ways to tell God you're grateful. A thankful heart is one that God looks upon with favor.

Seek His Face

Last, I'd encourage you to pray for *a move of God* in your team—that an unquenchable love for His presence would fill their hearts. Pray that they would be filled with a desire to bring a sound worthy of a King. That's why we aim for excellence and creativity. Both of those things are a demonstration of taking your craft seriously. The Holy Spirit is the ultimate giver of creativity. Excellence is what we bring to the table; it's our offering to Him. Pray for receptive hearts among your congregation, that God's presence would become the church's passion.

As my pastor Mark Batterson often says, "Prayer is the difference between the best you can do and the best God can do." I know whose best I want on my side. Prayer is the key. Let your leadership and worship life be first formed by a heart of prayer. Through the life and ways of Jesus, we see that prayer is in His very DNA. I close with our Savior's words in Matthew 21: "My house will be called a house of prayer." Let that be the case in our churches and in our homes. Amen.

Closing Thought

In Psalm 109, David gives us a great picture of what prayer is. He's facing a real struggle. Those in his inner circle have "opened their mouths against" him and spoken of him with "lying tongues." He even says, "[I]n return for my friendship they accuse me." I can think of little worse than offering friendship to someone only to receive judgment in return. David had every right to curse them to their faces. Instead, he talks to the Lord about it.

When he does, he gives us a little hint of the reality of prayer. In verse 4, the NIV translation has the phrase "But I am a man of prayer." Other translations have the words "But I am in prayer," but the literal Hebrew translation of this phrase is "But I am prayer."

Prayer is more than something we do. It is something we become. It's not meant to be a checklist item. Consider it to be that by which your spirit is alive. As breath is to lungs, prayer is to your spirit.

This gives even greater meaning to the apostle Paul's challenge to pray "without ceasing." Our end goal with prayer should be to remain in communion with the Spirit of God at all times, acknowledging Him in all our ways.

A mentor once shared with me that life is meant to be lived "in the plural." In every activity of life (especially worship ministry), there is never an "I" or "me" moment. Everything we do is a "we" and "us" moment. God is present in all of our conversations, car rides, teeth brushing, rehearsals, workout sessions. Even when you're sleeping, He's there. Maybe the best kind of prayer is simply that which never steps out of reach, ever tuned in to the Holy Spirit.

Clayton Brooks
Worship artist and songwriter
Founder, 12:1 Worship

CHAPTER 5

A Change of Heart

He came from a family that specialized in war. His father created torpedoes and other explosives for a living and did fairly well, so young Alfred went into the family business. He invented dynamite and established 90 armament factories to aid in the art of war. However, in an accident at one of these factories, his brother Ludvig and several others were tragically killed in an explosion. Several newspapers in error wrote Alfred's name in the obituary. One article had the headline "The Merchant of Death Is Dead." When Alfred read that, he couldn't bear the thought of the world remembering him as a warmonger and someone who only profited off of people dying. So he turned his life around. Some of us call this a "come to Jesus moment." From then on, Alfred vowed to live for a different cause. What was Alfred's last name, you may ask? Nobel, as in, the Nobel Peace Prize. In November 1895, he wrote in his will to give away 94 percent of his assets to the Nobel Prize Foundation, which would award those in the world who fought for the greater good of mankind through science, literature, and peace! In today's currency his fortune would be worth nearly $500 million. Instead of a legacy of war, he's known for a legacy of peace. Just another story proving it's *never* too late to be who you were meant to be. It's never too late for a change of heart!

The word "repent" might be one of the most misunderstood words in the Christian dictionary. The Greek word for "repentance" is *metanoia*. It means to have a change of heart, to turn around and walk in a new direction.

As we all know, you can ask for forgiveness and easily walk right back into your old life with your old sin habits. It doesn't make sense, but so many of us do this. It's like knowing the dangers of eating level-five Nashville hot chicken but going for it anyway. And you reap the consequences. (I'm not speaking from experience or anything.)

Saying "sorry" to God is only as good as the action that follows the word. Actions speak louder than words, right? As a church called to worship, we need to be a people whose words line up with our actions. As we sing and lead our songs of worship, we need to keep in mind Jesus' words in Matthew 15:8-9: "These people honor me with their lips, but their hearts are far from me. They worship me in vain; their teachings are merely human rules."

A huge chunk of the Psalms are prayers of repentance and songs of consecration. In our modern-day landscape of songs, I think we have a good amount of pump-up, victorious jams, but not a ton of songs that reflect a set-apart heart. This is a challenge for the songwriters and worship leaders out there. After all, it was David who wrote, "A broken and contrite heart you, God, will not despise." (Ps. 51:17)

A Story of Repentance

King David had a journey that gives us so many reference points as leaders today.

The life of David went from the pasture as a shepherd to the battle-field as a soldier to the palace as king. It's the story that Hollywood dreams are made of. And once David was on the throne, he had to wrestle the fight that all of us wrestle daily: pride vs. praise. David fought a lot of wars in his reign and won a lot of victories, but he got to the point in his life when he just wanted to coast, to take it easy.

> In the spring, at the time when kings go off to war, David sent Joab out with the king's men and the whole Israelite army. They destroyed the Ammonites and besieged Rabbah. But David remained in Jerusalem.
>
> One evening David got up from his bed and walked around on the roof of the palace. From the roof he saw a woman bath-ing. The woman was very beautiful, and David sent someone to find out about her. The man said, "She is Bathsheba, the daugh-

ter of Eliam and the wife of Uriah the Hittite." Then David sent messengers to get her. She came to him, and he slept with her. (Now she was purifying herself from her monthly uncleanness.) Then she went back home. The woman conceived and sent word to David, saying, "I am pregnant." (2 Sam 11:1-5)

This is a hard lesson to walk through, but as leaders we have a huge target on our backs. Just as there is a real God who is *for* you, so too there is a real enemy who is *against* you. Jesus came to give us life to the full, but the enemy comes to steal, kill, and destroy, according to John 10:10. The enemy uses tactics like temptation, pride, lies, and attacks on your mind, body, and soul. He does *not* want you to succeed in leading people to authentic encounters with God. Yet, so often we walk unknowingly into battle without any armor on. We can sometimes think that if we read the Bible three times a week and twice on Sunday, and if we listen to the Christian radio station exclusively, then we're impenetrable to attack. We have to be aware that sin is crouching at the door, waiting to take us out.

> You will be accepted if you do what is right. But if you refuse to do what is right, then watch out! Sin is crouching at the door, eager to control you. But you must subdue it and be its master. (Gen. 4:7, NLT)

In the New Testament, Peter wrote it this way:

> Stay alert! Watch out for your great enemy, the devil. He prowls around like a roaring lion, looking for someone to devour. Stand firm against him, and be strong in your faith. Remember that your family of believers all over the world is going through the same kind of suffering you are. (1 Pet. 5:8-9, NLT)

The enemy is lurking about, waiting for a chance to creep in. Yeah, he's a creeper. But here's Peter's advice: don't give him a foothold. Don't open that door. Don't let him in. Resist the enemy, and he will flee! Stand firm in your faith.

See, David gave the enemy a foothold. When he fell into his epic sin with Bathsheba, the chapter opens up like this: "At the time when kings go off to war." David should have been out with his army, but he stayed behind. And when you stay behind, and you get alone, and you don't do what you're supposed to be doing, then that's a perfect opportunity for the enemy to slip in. That's precisely when David jacked up. Alone, bored, I'm sure his thoughts started to eat at his mind. Pride overcame his praise. He looked to his selfish interests over God's. He wanted instant gratification instead of thinking through the long-term consequences. And there are always consequences to our actions. Even with repentance and forgiveness, there are still results that play out from those choices.

Bathsheeba told David she was pregnant. And Maury Povich showed up to the palace and said, "You *are* the father!" The tabloids in Israel were buzzing. David knew he was in trouble, and he did what most powerful men in his position would probably do—he covered it up. But here's the deal, *you can't cover up anything from a God who sees everything.*

You've read the story. David had Uriah killed in battle and took Bathsheeba to be his wife. And everything is all good. Right? Not quite. Now throughout the Old Testament, God spoke to His people primarily through the prophets, and the prophet of Israel during David's reign was a guy named Nathan.

> The Lord sent Nathan to David. When he came to him, he said, "There were two men in a certain town, one rich and the other poor. The rich man had a very large number of sheep and cattle, but the poor man had nothing except one little ewe lamb he had bought. He raised it, and it grew up with him and his children. It shared his food, drank from his cup and even slept in his arms. It was like a daughter to him. Now a traveler came to the rich man, but the rich man refrained from taking one of his own sheep or cattle to prepare a meal for the traveler who had come to him. Instead, he took the ewe lamb that belonged to the poor man and prepared it for the one who had come to him."
>
> David burned with anger against the man and said to Nathan, "As surely as the Lord lives, the man who did this must die! He must pay for that lamb four times over, because he did such a thing and had no pity."
>
> Then Nathan said to David, "You are the man!" (2 Sam. 12:1-7)

Listen to the Voice of Conviction

Consecration and conviction go hand in hand. The word "consecration" means "set apart." Don't be like the others. Don't listen to the way of culture over the still small voice of the Holy Spirit. That's where conviction becomes action. As Billy Graham said, "It's God's job to judge, the Holy Spirit's job to convict, and my job to love." The Holy Spirit needs to be the loudest voice in our lives. If we ever want to have anything worth saying throughout our days, we need to be setting apart time to spend in the quiet presence of the Lord so that He can speak to us.

In the story in 2 Samuel, the prophet Nathan was that voice of conviction. Since the floodgates opened at Pentecost, followers of Jesus have the unlimited voice of the Holy Spirit guiding us, directing us, and nudging us in the way that God wants us to go. The enemy condemns; the Spirit convicts. Conviction is a good thing. David listened to the voice of conviction. He could have easily had Nathan thrown out, killed, or imprisoned. But he knew in his heart that Nathan was saying the right stuff. The Holy Spirit will convict you of what you know to be wrong, what you know isn't truth. In and of ourselves, we won't find the answers. We have to tune in to the voice of the Spirit and listen to what God is saying. And when we've made a mistake, we need to repent.

Repentance Starts with Recognition

Second Samuel 12:13 tells us, "Then David said to Nathan, 'I have sinned against the Lord.'" David recognized his sin and confessed to the wrong. In his book *The Beauty of the In-Between*, pastor Matthew Nelson writes about three kings: Saul, David, and Solomon—that only one of them had a story that ended well. Saul, who was Israel's first king, had some big mess-ups, but he never owned up to them. He blamed everyone else and always avoided repentance. Solomon, David's son, lived a righteous life for most of his days, but at the end turned away from the Lord and followed the foreign gods of his many wives. But David, whose story ended in peace and prosperity, had a repentant heart. When he messed up, he admitted it and made a course correction. And after the episode with Bathsheba, in his repentance David wrote one of the most famous psalms, Psalm 51:

> Have mercy on me, O God,
>   according to your unfailing love;
>   according to your great compassion
>   blot out my transgressions.
> Wash away all my iniquity
>   and cleanse me from my sin.

Here's what we have to get in our times of worship: *repentance leads to restoration!* We need songs of repentance, and we need to lead our congregations to a place of restoration! From brokenness to wholeness. From hurting to healing.

David sang, "Restore to me the joy of your salvation." It's hard to have joy when you have unconfessed sin in your life, isn't it? Sin eats at you, it creeps at the door, and it eventually moves in and overstays its welcome. But when you repent and confess your sin, it's a literal weight being lifted off your heart, and you kick the unwelcome guest out of your heart, mind, and soul. The people in our churches need to know that there is *joy* to be found in the presence of God. His joy changes everything, and I believe there's a shortage of joy in the world these days. We have a record number of anxiety prescriptions today, and fear seems to be the major selling point of every news channel. Suicide has taken way too many lives of people who felt there was no other way out. There *is* a way out of depression and anxiety, and it's called the gospel. Jesus is our joy. And the road to joy is a heart of repentance so that the weight of sin that we carry can be lifted off.

Bishop T. D. Jakes said, "You cannot have revival if you do not have repentance." We all want to see revival in the church, especially in the realm of worship. I believe that revival comes on the coattails of an authentic move of the Spirit in worship. But to get to experience the revival that this world desperately needs, we need to return to the heart of God. That is what repentance is. A literal 180-degree turn back to the heart of God. My personal prayer is this: "Lord, let revival start in me. God, whatever it is in me, if it's not of You, take it away. If I've placed *my* goals above *Thy* goals, redirect me." Much like David wrote, we need to sing, "Create in me a pure heart O God, and renew a stead-fast spirit within me." Repentance is not stepping back into your old ways.

A Change of Heartburn

I mentioned hot chicken earlier in this chapter, and that's something I've been a fan of since moving to Nashville. However, these days I have to be a little more cautious in what I eat. A couple Christmases ago, while out of town on vacation, my wife and I had a bit of a scare. I hadn't felt right all day, and I was experiencing a tightness in my chest. I thought I was having a heart attack! We checked my blood pressure, and it was off the charts. So we rushed to the emergency room and saw a doctor. Turns out, my symptoms were reflective of severe acid reflux, heartburn, and a small ulcer. The doctor asked what my diet was, and without hesitation I shared the laundry list of quality foods that I ate on the regular: fast food burgers, spicy ethnic foods, lots of fried foods, including (you guessed it) Nashville hot chicken almost every week! It wasn't rocket science what the problem was. I needed a major shift in my eating habits. It would have been foolish to leave that hospital and step right back into the old diet. But if you want to see different results, you can't keep doing the same thing! That's the literal definition of insanity, right? So my wife helped me make some changes, and I'm happy to say I haven't had an episode like that since that day. If you want to get healthy, you can't keep eating like a slob! Make decisions that will accomplish the results you're after. It works in the spiritual sense too.

Sing of the Cross

David's song was obviously written in the BC era, foreshadowing the coming Savior. Jesus, the friend of sinners, would come to meet us in the mess and become our salvation on the cross. As we lead worship songs of repentance, let's point our congregations to the power of the cross and the restoring hope of Jesus, the One who sticks closer than a brother. There's something about a song that cuts straight through the layers we've built up and gives us a chance to sing our deepest emotions. We need more songs of repentance so that we can lead more people to consecration. Psalm 51 is that kind of prayer. Worship songs are prayers put to melody.

It was about 20 years ago that Matt Redman wrote one of the greatest worship songs of all time: "Heart of Worship." But before the song became a staple in worship sets across the globe, it was written for his home church, Soul Survivor, in Watford, England. The church was going through a time of apathy in their musical worship, so the pastor did something brave. He removed the band and PA system from their Sunday morning experience. They stripped away the things they counted on to manufacture an experience and had a season when people were kind of forced to sing out their own songs and prayers—and it led to a fresh encounter. No lights, no band, just pure honest worship that radiated throughout the church. Piece by piece, with the change of heart, they added elements back into their service, realizing that worship didn't depend on any of those things, but it was about a people praising their King. Matt took this season to his room and wrote these words:

> I'm sorry, Lord, for the things I've made it
> When it's all about you, it's all about you

The heart of worship is humble and broken before a King. It is repentant and longs to be consecrated for the service of the kingdom of God.

What's Your Motive?

I can remember a time when I wanted to give up songwriting and worship leading altogether. I was very discouraged, even though I was in a position that many worship leaders dream of. I had been asked to take part in a major label album that brought together leaders of a movement, and it would be released on a pretty large-scale platform. I was excited, until I showed my songs to the label reps. They seemed to like everyone else's songs but told me I needed to write something better. This made me question my abilities and sent me on a mad scramble, chasing the ever elusive hit, only to find myself in the worst writer's block I've ever experienced. I couldn't seem to write a decent melody or find any inspirational lyrics. I had hit a wall. It was maddening, because at the time I was writing a song nearly every day! Now I couldn't put together two lines.

Around this time, our church staff went to a conference in Atlanta. At some point during the conference one of the speakers got up and said, "I want to take a moment and just listen to the Spirit of God speak." He encouraged us to pray, in a room of thousands, and tune everything out to just hear the Father's voice. As I prayed, I felt God whisper to me, "Would you write a song if I was the only one to hear it?" It broke me. I knew in that moment my motives for worship leading and songwriting were in the wrong place. I wasn't broken and contrite; I was prideful and entitled. I thought that God in a sense "owed" me a song of revival because I had decided to be a worship leader. What a backward way of thinking!

So in that moment, surrounded by thousands of other church leaders, I felt like it was just me and Jesus in the room. And I put the dream on the altar. I prayed that He would just give me a new heart, and whatever He wanted to do with the gifts that He'd given me, I would yield to His will! And as God often does, He resurrected the dream with a pure motive, and He gave me a new reason to sing and write and the songs to go along with it. One of those songs ended up being a co-write with the other worship leaders on the project, "To Honor You." It's without a doubt one of my favorite songs I've ever had a hand in. And just like the title, it wasn't about me; it was all about bringing Jesus the fame and glory He alone deserves.

D. L. Moody is quoted as saying, "The world has yet to see what God will do with a man fully consecrated to Him." Throughout the Bible, we see the word "wholeheartedly." It means exactly what you think it does.

Worship is an atmosphere where God restores, heals, and sets free. But He can only heal what you expose. He doesn't take things from us forcefully. With my own kids, if they mess up, I want them to come and tell me, because forgiveness and love wait on the other side of repentance. To be honest, I grew up thinking that when we come to church, we are supposed to leave all of our baggage at the door. But the truth is, God wants us to bring it to Him and lay it at the foot of the cross. The beautiful exchange of the gospel is that Jesus takes our mess and gives us His beauty. He gives us righteousness for our rags. In Matthew 11:28-30, Jesus says, "Come to me, all you who are weary and burdened, and I will give you rest. Take my yoke upon you and learn from me, for I am gentle and humble in heart, and you will find rest for your souls. For my yoke is easy and my burden is light."

That sounds almost too good to be true, but that's the message of the gospel. He sets captives free, gives salvation to the sinner, and brings the exile to a place of restoration! This is the Jesus we get to worship and lead others in worshiping!

Let repentance start in you, and then live out of the freedom! If there's anything you've been holding back, anything that's been eating at your soul, now is the time to lay it at the feet of Jesus.

What do you need to repent of today? What do you need to confess?

David recognized his sin but he didn't stay in it. When you come to God broken, He can put you back together, and then He can mobilize you as an instrument of healing for others. Your scars can be a story that helps others. But remember, you can't be much help to others if you haven't properly healed. Lead from scars, not wounds. It's like trying to play basketball on a sprained ankle. You'll hurt your team *and* yourself! Let repentance be your song and consecration your mission!

I encourage you to end this chapter with a prayer. It could look a lot like Psalm 51. Take a moment and read that amazing song of David. And I am praying as I write that God would restore the joy of your salvation!

Closing Thought

Repentance and consecration. Could there be a more timely call to the Church? "Then if my people who are called by my name will humble themselves and pray and seek my face and turn from their wicked ways, I will hear from heaven and will forgive their sins and restore their land" (2 Chron. 7:14). This is the heartbeat behind NCC Worship, the worship ministry that Kurtis and I stewarded and led at National Community Church in Washington, DC. It became so core to our ministry that we got tattoos with our "714" logo. I have had the honor of leading the charge with NCC Worship after KP moved back to Nashville to launch Bridges Nashville.

Second Chronicles 7:14 is a beautiful and powerful promise of scripture given by God to King Solomon as he completed and dedicated the Temple. Solomon's passion for the house of God reminds me of another man of God who had a passion for the presence. Joshua was a mighty man of God and a protégé to Moses. Joshua had the privilege of accompanying Moses into the Tabernacle. "The Lord would speak to Moses face to face, as one speaks to a friend. Then Moses would return to the camp, but his young aide Joshua son of Nun did not leave the tent" (Exod. 33:11). Joshua certainly knew the presence of God and certainly demonstrated the magnitude of what God can do through someone consecrated.

Early in my worship-leading journey, I had the privilege of being on a Skype call with John Mark McMillan, who spoke on consecration and leadership. I was so impacted by that conversation that I left with a new charge: for every hour I would spend onstage leading worship in front of people, I would spend two hours offstage worshiping God in my prayer closet. Some seasons have been better than others but one thing has become clear: who I am in the secret place, both the holy and sinful, will be revealed in the spotlight. My prayer for you and me is that we will continue to cultivate the character that will sustain our calling, and that only happens through a life of repentance and consecration.

Chris Douglas
Worship director, National Community Church

CHAPTER 6
A Church That Looks Like Heaven

Martin Luther King, Jr., once said, "Sunday 11 a.m. is our most segregated hour of the week."

As I write this chapter, our nation is in crisis. It's 2020, and in the midst of dealing with a global virus called COVID-19, another ugly virus has shown its face in sickening ways: racism. Headlines are filled with peaceful protests, not-so-peaceful riots, cities divided, politicians yelling, and everyone's opinions on full blast. Yet there are also hopeful conversations and churches leaning into reconciliation. There are movements of healing and relationships forming. When we read the Scriptures, we see a book filled with God's plan for our unity.

Psalm 133 says that it's pleasing to God when we live united, and His blessing is in it. In John 17, Jesus prayed for His disciples and all the disciples who would come to dwell in unity. Paul wrote these words to the early church in 1 Corinthians 1:10: "I appeal to you, dear brothers and sisters, by the authority of our Lord Jesus Christ, to live in harmony with each other. Let there be no divisions in the church. Rather, be of one mind, united in thought and purpose."

The Holy Spirit, whom Jesus left behind, is a Spirit who unites the people of God, according to Ephesians 4. It's absolutely clear that God wants His kids to get along, to be for each other, and to change the world by our love for one another. And yet when we look at the news reels, the media, and social media, we see a lot of the opposite—division. People would rather prove their point than hear someone else's side. For these times, I'm challenged by Jesus' brother James: "My dear brothers and sisters, take note of this: Everyone should be quick to listen, slow to speak, and slow to become angry." (Jas. 1:19)

So in the realm of worship and worship leading, how do we not just manage this tension but also solve this problem? One word: "family." When you look at the kingdom of God, the descriptor that overwhelmingly fits what the Church should be is "family." We can't live out those nearly 60 "one another" commands in the New Testament if we're separated and segregated. We have to actually be *with* one another, *for* one another, and *love* one another—and not just the one another that looks like us, thinks like us, sings like us, plays like us, and listens to the worship playlists we prefer. Growth is uncomfortable, but I can guarantee that the last time you had a breakthrough in your life, it followed on the heels of being uncomfortable. This chapter will stretch you, it will make you uncomfortable, and it will cause you to think outside the box, and therefore grow. I think that's the reason you picked up this book, so let's continue.

Several years ago I had the opportunity to lead worship with several worship leaders at General Council. It's a conference put on by the Assemblies of God, where churches from all across the world come together to worship, hear from the movement leaders, and connect with other members of the body of Christ. I will never forget the sound of 20,000 believers lifting up praise to the God of every nation. It was a beautiful sight and probably one of the closest moments on this side of eternity that what heaven looks like! When people from every tribe, tongue, and nation come together to worship Jesus, that is a mirror of what happens in heaven.

> . . . that at the name of Jesus every knee should bow, of those in heaven, and of those on earth, and of those under the earth, and that every tongue should confess that Jesus Christ is Lord, to the glory of God the Father. (Phil. 2:10)

> After this I looked, and behold, a great multitude that no one could number, from every nation, from all tribes and peoples and languages, standing before the throne and before the Lamb, clothed in white robes, with palm branches in their hands. (Rev. 7:9)

These two verses point to the very reason we need a chapter like this in a book on worship. If we want to live in Jesus' prayer "on earth as it is in heaven," then we need to promote the type of worship that exists in heaven. The gospel is non-exclusive, and Jesus invites everyone to the table. It is His desire that *all* would come into the family of God, and in turn worship and be a part of the kingdom of God. I believe that every church has a unique vision, calling, and purpose that will streamline who they draw and who they reach. We all have our lane to run in, no doubt. I also believe that there are some barriers that could be torn down that keep people from stepping through our doors. You can't be everything to everyone, but you can have a style of worship that is multidimensional and not just one flavor. I've never tasted a meal made of one ingredient that tasted that good. I've never seen a painting with one color that was that artistic. And I think worship is too big and beautiful to box in.

Many Flavors

This is an area in which I've been challenged and have had to grow in since the moment I started leading worship at 13 years old in my dad's small non-denominational church. As a teenager leading mostly 30-, 40-, and 50-year-olds in worship, I was way out of my comfort zone. You could see the generational gap from a mile away. I was a teenager wearing Airwalks and JNCOs (30 points for anyone who had a pair), leading a congregation in button-ups and blazers. Yet even in that great divide, we came together to worship. Why? Because of the least common denominator, or perhaps I should say the *great* common denominator: Jesus.

We came together in worship because we all realized that Jesus was the name we were lifting high, not any of our own. Jesus was the King in the room, and whatever, however we worshiped Him, that was the point. Now, I had to find songs and even write songs that brought people together on the same page. Honestly, that's one of the goals in leading worship: to get everyone to the table. We know it's the Lord who serves the meal, but we can set the table well and invite people in communion with Jesus to have a seat.

As my worship-leading journey went on, I found myself leading worship in college at Campus Crusade for Christ at Virginia Tech, where nearly every song was foreign to me. This was the first time I heard songs by Chris Tomlin (was I living under a rock or something?). Later on down the road, I had the opportunity to lead worship in Nashville at Oasis Church. Hands down, Oasis was one of the most ethnically diverse and generationally minded churches I've ever been to. In a worship set, we would lead a Hillsong, then a Black Gospel song, followed by a '90s throwback, with a Spanish chorus thrown in for good measure. I was stretched in my leadership and learned to lead songs by Ricardo Sanchez, Jonathan Stockstill, and Israel Houghton. It was an incredible worship experience that brought in so many flavors and did so with style and grace—not to mention some of Nashville's finest musicians! It's not easy to pull off the musicianship behind some of those songs.

When I moved to Washington, DC, in 2010, I was challenged again at National Community Church, where on any given Sunday in any given row you could have people from 20 different faith backgrounds worshiping together—Pentecostals next to Catholics next to agnostics. DC is a giant melting pot, with people from every nation, every background. We had un-churched, de-churched, re-churched all sitting next to one another. It was incredible! Children were a part of the worship service too, which opened my eyes to the fact that there is no Junior Jesus. So I started writing worship songs that kids could gravitate toward, and soon I had my own children. God was growing my passion for multigenerational worship alongside multicultural worship. It was here that I learned to lead hymns for the first time.

Now in my more recent years of church planting and leading worship in Nashville, we are experimenting with new sounds and leaning into the Country flavor that is the DNA of our city. All of this goes to show you that leading worship is not and should never be boring! We worship a genius God who has more flavors than Baskin Robbins. It should inspire us to expand our worship repertoire!

Generational

Your church may have way more young adults than senior citizens. You probably have a certain ethnic makeup as well. That's okay. I think that what makes the body of Christ so amazing is that each part does what it's called to do. First Corinthians 12:20 says, "As it is, there are many parts, but one body."

In your worship service, you want people to know that Jesus calls people from every walk of life and that He died for every generation. We often say this phrase at my church: "Every face has a name, every name has a story, and every story matters to God."

The Bible talks often about generational community. Deuteronomy 6 speaks to the importance of generations passing on what they have in God. The Bible was passed down orally from one generation to the next. They didn't have computers or even books in the way we have today. You had to get different age groups together so that faith could be transferred. The Psalms show us how songs were passed down to teach the next generation of God's faithfulness.

> . . . for I will speak to you in a parable.
> I will teach you hidden lessons from our past—
> stories we have heard and known,
>   stories our ancestors handed down to us.
> We will not hide these truths from our children;
>   we will tell the next generation
> about the glorious deeds of the Lord,
>   about his power and his mighty wonders.
> For he issued his laws to Jacob;
>   he gave his instructions to Israel.
> He commanded our ancestors
>   to teach them to their children,
> so the next generation might know them—
>   even the children not yet born—
>   and they in turn will teach their own children.
> So each generation should set its hope anew on God,
>   not forgetting his glorious miracles
>   and obeying his commands. (Ps. 78:2-7)

Know Your Identity

Have you ever thought about who is in your church? I hope you can answer that. Side note: you can't *know* your church if you spend all your time in a Green Room before and after service. Get out in the lobby and greet people! You'll always be a better worship leader if you know the people you're called to lead! I tell all of our worship team that we are also on the hospitality team! Find out who is coming to your church. That will also show you who is missing and who you need to be inviting!

One of the best books I've ever read on church planting is Rick Warren's *Purpose Driven Church*. He shares how he quickly understood who Saddleback Church was reaching, based on who they were going after, and then they designed their worship experience to connect with that demographic. I've become friends with John Cassetto, the Global Worship Pastor at Saddleback, and I love his passion to stretch their teams culturally and stylistically. He's passionate about the world connecting with Jesus. When they started as one location, they knew whom they were reaching, and now as they have a church presence all over the globe, they also know how to reach and connect people in worship to Jesus.

If you have a church of mostly families and middle-aged people, doing an all Hillsong Young & Free set list with synths and drum machines probably won't connect well—much like doing an all Keith Green worship set list might not connect with a college-aged church body. If you are anything like the majority of churches in the world, you probably have a good mix of different age groups and backgrounds, but you also probably have a particular demographic that you're connecting with. So find songs that can connect with that mix! Don't lock yourself into only leading one type of song, because that will get routine, predictable, and boring—three adjectives that should never be associated with Church. The other side of the coin is not going all over the place with your style so that no one can ever catch on and join in. Your team will be confused, and so too will your church. It takes a beautiful balance.

What is the culture of your church? Some churches feel like walking into a pop concert while others feel like walking into a silent film. There are challenges and opportunities, strengths and weaknesses with every style, but you have to match the culture and overall vision of your church with the worship life. For instance, if your church is heavy on video and has a high production emphasis, an all acoustic and piano worship set might feel a little disjointed. The same thing goes if your church meets in a century-old church building with stained glass windows but you're leading worship on a keytar. Hey, I love a good keytar, but is the culture of the church tied into the culture of worship you're called to steward as a worship leader?

Let me take a quick left turn and be the old guy in the room advocating for leading hymns just a moment. Colossians 3:16 says, "Let the message of Christ dwell among you richly as you teach and admonish one another with all wisdom through psalms, hymns, and songs from the Spirit, singing to God with gratitude in your hearts." Hymns have been around for a very long time. Many of the hymns we have today are wells of theology, with lyrics and melodies that have stood the test of time. They were written to connect with people who didn't have the Internet, iPhones, or Spotify. They could be sung anywhere, with or without musical instruments. Many of the hymns written hundreds of years ago were based off pop culture songs and bar tunes, because that's how they reached people.

The lyrics to the hymns will challenge your faith. And the stories behind the songs will blow your mind.

Think about this: there are songs and sermons from previous generations that are still speaking into life today. There are messages and songs preached today that will live on past our lifetime. The same goes with books!

Music transcends time and space. If you still need a reason to implement hymns in your worship culture, chew on this: Jesus was a fan of hymns. Matthew 26:30 tells us that right after communion, before Jesus and the disciples headed out to the Mount of Olives, they sang a hymn.

We shouldn't get so caught up in the trends of today that we neglect the shoulders we're standing on. There are so many albums being released every month now with so many churches releasing music all the time. I love that because churches are capturing the stories and testimonies in their house through songs that will live on! But sometimes it feels like it's hard to keep up. Oftentimes I feel like I'm trying to stay afloat and stay with the latest hit song. But don't forget that there's a whole world of hymns out there that have been sung for hundreds of years, long before ProPresenter was around to project lyrics on a screen.

When thinking about the people who fill your church, consider that everyone has value and needs a place to worship. So don't get so lost in the art of music that you lose the heart of worship. Make sure your church can *sing* the song! Sometimes we pick songs that are melodically hard to follow and lyrically confusing. Here's the deal: if *you* have trouble grabbing ahold of a song as a worship leader, then I can guarantee that the average non-musical person in your church will have trouble.

Pick songs in keys that people can participate in, not just spectate. And make sure the lyrics you're singing are theologically on point and not so poetic and artistic that people are left scratching their hands instead of raising their hands.

If your Sundays don't lend to a multigenerational and multicultural style of worship, I'd encourage you to find places and ways to make room for that. I'm sure you've often heard song requests and different people wanting to do different songs and styles. Try to make opportunities to honor that, when it's in your power to do so. I've led electronica EDM-styled worship nights with a DJ onstage to reach a younger demographic. I've been involved in all-acoustic hymn nights. I've been a part of Black Gospel concerts where I was the only white guy in the room. I've had a blast in every environment—and each time I come out a better worship leader. Mark Batterson has a phrase: "bump into other people's anointing." We grow when we get in different environments! If you know of another church that is doing something unique in their worship culture, go and join them for a service! You'll probably come away with a friend, and definitely a greater appreciation for the body of Christ!

It's Deference over Preference

"Be devoted to one another in love. Honor one another above yourselves" (Romans 12:10).

Dr. David Manner said, "Deference is the agreement that although we may not always love the music of our children and grandchildren . . . we love our children and grandchildren. Deference is the willingness to set aside our preferences for the good of those children and grandchildren. Multigenerational worship will occur when the only battle is over who can offer/give the most instead of who deserves/demands the most."

When we choose personal preference over what our church needs, we're going to miss the vision and the very mission of Jesus. We live in a very divided world. People separate themselves based on social status, political preference, economic standing, and many other factors. As the Church, we're not supposed to look like the world. What if you could fuse those separate worlds into something harmonious that brings everyone to the same table? I don't think Jesus' desire was to see people only connecting with their age groups, or people only hanging out with others who agree with their point of view. Jesus crossed cultural lines with His parables like the Good Samaritan and the Prodigal Son. He showed honor to those who least expected it and gave dignity to those the world cast aside. He valued women in a day and age when they were thought of as property. He hung out with lepers and chose a crew of misfits as disciples.

Personally, as a pastor, I want people to cross-pollinate different viewpoints and backgrounds, because we sharpen each other's faith. I want the wisdom of older generations to connect with the passion of the younger generation. I want the experience of families to inspire the drive of our young adults. Worship is a form of discipleship, as it's teaching theology and shaping the way we see God. This is so important! When you have children worshiping with their parents, and seniors worshiping with teenagers, family is happening! When you have stories and prayers being shared across timelines, you can see identity and faith being built. Like at a family dinner table on Thanksgiving, identity happens when the family of God comes together.

Unity > Diversity

One year, my dad gave me an Ancestry DNA kit for my birthday. I lost it when we moved from DC to Nashville and found it a couple years later. Thank God it didn't expire and I could still take the test. It was pretty wild to see the combination of cultures that I come from and how they all play a little piece in who I am today. Diversity is important, and as I've said many times in this chapter, the body of Christ isn't one color, one style, one flavor. We are *many* parts, *one* body. That word "one" leans into the word "unity."

Sometimes in our conversations we focus so much on diversity that we forget it's more about unity. Diversity honors the differences in the room, and that is huge; but unity brings us all together with a common purpose, and that's more of the emphasis we see in Scripture.

> There is neither Jew nor Gentile, neither slave nor free, nor is there male and female, for you are all one in Christ Jesus. (Gal. 3:28)

> How good and pleasant it is when God's people live together in unity! (Ps. 133:1)

In both Philippians 2:10 and Revelation 7, the verses referenced at the beginning of this chapter, the focus isn't on the tribes and tongues; rather, it's on Jesus. So do your songs and your style of worship point to Him over everything else? Are you enabling everyone to sing, or are you leaving behind the people you're called to lead? Anytime we can remove barriers to unity, we are stepping in the right direction. The gospel invites everyone!

Practically Speaking

At the church I planted, Bridges Nashville, we certainly don't have everything figured out, and we're learning constantly. The moment we have everything perfect, I will let you know, but I don't see that happening anytime soon. But there are steps we took and that you can take to grow in this area. For instance, we have four or five different worship leaders with very different backgrounds and preferences, but we all come together in choosing the songs that we lead on a Sunday. We have a worship leader who is 19 and another in their 40s. We have Gospel, Folk, Country, Rock, and Pop-styled voices at the table. When you have multiple voices at the table, you get a broader scope of wisdom and experience. Great ingredients make great meals!

Focus more on *who* you're worshiping than on *how* you're worshiping. Here's what I mean: it's not so much the song style but the content! Also, don't forget that multigenerational includes kids. If you do kids church separately, then are they singing songs that engage them in worshiping Jesus? Kids need to see older generations worshiping so that they can be discipled in worship. My dad always said, "Things are more caught than taught." Kids will catch it when they see it. We have children join us in the sanctuary for the opening worship. When we do house church, families can worship together, and then before the message the kids are led to kids church. The young ones have the opportunity to learn with their peers and their family.

You Can't Force It, But You Can Shape It

When I was in college, my summers were spent working a landscaping job with my uncle. There were several jobs where we had to plant grass to grow in a particular pattern in a yard. So we first had to set out a pattern, then shape where we would plant the sod, and then set barriers in place where we didn't want it to grow. It was shaping the way the grass would grow and thus laying out the vision of that particular yard. We couldn't *make* the grass grow; only God moving through the nature He created could do that. What we could control was the shape and how we planted.

Maybe you catch my drift. You cannot force a multicultural, multi-generational worship movement in your church. I've seen churches try this and you can smell phony a mile away. Worship teams don't step into their full potential, congregations end up confused, and the pastors usually end up frustrated. Most times that we try to take control of a situation, by default we remove God's hand from it. We need to work in tandem with the Spirit of God. If you want to take an authentic step in this direction, begin by praying for the right people to steward it. My questions to anyone in leadership who wants to have a greater level of unity with generational and cultural worship are, Who do you have in the room? Who is on your team? Who are your co-leaders? Make sure you don't have all clones and mirror images of yourself. Surround yourself with different thinkers with different backgrounds, and invite the other voices to the table.

Jesus had a diverse team—from fishermen to tax collectors. I'm sure the dinner conversation at His table could get pretty heated. You know what happens when iron sharpens iron, right? Sparks fly from the friction. It's a simple byproduct of getting different minds together. But Jesus wasn't interested in a one-flavored type of church. He was a blessing to *all* people, according to the Abrahamic covenant back in Genesis!

The healthiest and strongest worship teams I've been a part of, both leading and serving under others' leadership, were teams with worship leaders who looked different, sounded different, and thought differently.

A few years back, I was in a conversation with a worship team that wondered if there should be an age cap on the worship team. To be honest, it felt wrong, but we were asking the question about what kind of culture we were creating. I mean, in total transparency, you just don't see a lot of middle-aged folks or senior citizens onstage in the music videos that are being promoted in the music industry. (If you're squirming in your seat right now, that's the point.) The church I was a part of had a congregation that saw all sections of life crossing, and at the end of the day, we knew the stage needed to reflect our church. So we decided to have all ages welcome on the team. It only made the team stronger. We had people who were more experienced in life discipling the younger musicians on our team. We had after-church lunches where stories and traditions were shared. It was amazing. It was the body of Christ.

When it comes to style, it's great for your team to know you're not just locked in on your own favorite style but that you're open to growing. It'll stretch you as a leader and also stretch your team. I like to compare learning worship songs and styles to a swimmer. A swimmer may have their particular type of stroke that they excel in, like the backstroke or butterfly, but many high-level swimmers know how to do nearly every style.

You could take a Gospel song, and although your team isn't able to sing the layers of harmonies or complex keyboard runs, you still give it a go and adapt it to your team. With an older hymn, you might bring it up to a modern style with newer instrumentation and take out some of the augmented and diminished chords.

With a synth pop song, you could add an acoustic guitar or substitute the six pads with a piano.

It's about tackling new things and not being afraid of the challenge.

Grow Yourself

Simply put, as a worship leader it's about growing and expanding your base, spiritually and practically. By leading hymns, you step into a tradition of worship hundreds of years old. By singing psalms in your worship set, you're teaching Scripture. By leading other styles of music, you're expanding the worship language in your church and opening eyes, breaking down walls, and choosing the sound of heaven over the safety of tradition.

In the spirit of multigenerational worship, have someone older pouring into you, and find someone younger than yourself that you can pour into. You are a cultivator of environments, and the more you can do to point toward kingdom family, the better. Discipleship is the fruit of multigenerational worship. I love seeing people come together to encourage and inspire one another in faith. "One generation commends your works to another; they tell of your mighty acts" (Ps. 145:4).

In the spirit of multicultural worship, bump into someone else's anointing! Have a conversation with a worship leader from another background and go and worship with them! If you're a songwriter, write with those who might look and think differently than you. Your songs will be better! Challenge yourself to grow and learn. It's not easy. None of this chapter is. To be completely honest, following Jesus isn't easy. If it was, He would've left out that whole part about carrying our cross (see Matt. 16:24). It's not easy but it is simple. And you have the Holy Spirit to help you. Don't settle for easy; reach for the Kingdom. The Church is called to build bridges, not burn them. How can you bring people from different sides of the aisle together, to sit at the table? "So then, let us aim for harmony in the church and try to build each other up" (Rom. 14:19).

Closing Thought

For most of my childhood, I remember being the outsider. The charismatic services at the all-Black church I attended in Memphis, Tennessee, felt like home on Sunday but then seemed drastically foreign to my predominantly white high school on Monday morning. Clothing and hairstyles differed, along with slang, music, and lunch meals. The perfect picture of my mosaic upbringing would be the days I wore a FUBU shirt with my Birkenstock sandals!

Today, as a worship pastor, I empathize with people stuck in the middle aisle, not knowing which dominant position to take in controversial issues, or how to connect with different cultures and perspectives. I know what it feels like to be paralyzed, longing for a bridge between black and white, old and young, rich and poor, left and right.

What is God's answer to this? In addition to what Kurtis has already shared, I will offer these two pillars based on Scripture: (1) relationship through reconciliation (Eph. 2 and 1 Cor. 12) and (2) responsibility through representation (Titus 1). A real relationship is proven with sacrificial action, and effective responsibility is empowered by intentional delegation.

We will not grow in developing diversity in our churches until we intimately know, touch, love, and even promote those not exactly like us. Although colorful faces onstage and multilingual songs are helpful and needed, we must prioritize more meals and conversations, schedule targeted prayer services, plan strategic meetings, and recognize and honor others' points of view. May diversity live in our dining rooms and at our conference room tables. This is where we will see the beauty of difference and reflect the heart of God.

Kurtis, thank you for pushing God's message forward in this area. May our generation witness a miraculous and monumental shift in the area of diversity and equity, in Jesus' name.

Dwan Hill
Grammy-winning producer/songwriter
Worship pastor

CHAPTER 7

Praise Is the Anthem

Five hundred points if you can recite the entire National Anthem lyrics from memory. If you're like most of the country, you can probably get a few lines in, but then you start substituting words like "whose broad stripes and bright stars" with "who bought strikes and light scars." Or maybe you just start mouthing "watermelon" (the oldest trick in the book when you forget lyrics) as the anthem is being played over the intercom at a baseball game. I remember when I was asked to sing the anthem at a major event in DC. It was terrifying! There are many places you can get some grace on forgetting the words to the National Anthem, but our nation's capital is not one of them!

That song has been sung (and butchered) at sports stadiums, political events, classrooms, and many other gatherings for the last 100 years. It was written by a lawyer in his mid-30s named Francis Scott Key, after he witnessed the British Navy attack America during the battle of 1812. He was inspired by our flag, which at the time had only 15 stars and 15 stripes. It flew triumphantly at the end of the battle as a sign of victory. Before it was a song, it was a poem titled "The Defence of Fort M'Henry." Ironically enough, it was put to the tune of a British songwriter's melody. The song would come to be known as "The Star Spangled Banner." You could easily say the lyrics and they would hold weight, but when you put it to a melody, it takes on a different shape altogether; suddenly life, emotion, heart, and power are breathed into the words. Saying, "And the rocket's red glare," is one thing, but sing it and suddenly it takes on a whole new level of inspiration. An anthem is defined as "an uplifting song identified with a particular group, body, or cause." In this case it's a song that unified a new nation.

There are songs that become anthems in life. They become special moments that we never forget. Any time I hear Allison Kraus's "When You Say Nothing at All," it takes me back to sophomore year of college when I met my wife. She asked me to teach her to play the guitar line of that song. Let's just say, we didn't get too far in the lesson. Now married more than 17 years, I'm thankful for that song!

There are worship songs that become altar moments in our lives. After all, worship is the soundtrack to our conversations with God. Just hearing the first few bars of "Shout to the Lord" transports me back to my early days leading worship in my dad's small church in Virginia, playing on a Kurzweil keyboard. Music is the universal language. It can take us to moments and places in our past. God knew what He was doing when He created music.

Song is a gift from the Father to connect us to His heart. Melodies help us express what we want to say. In fact, sometimes we can only sing what we really want to say. If you've ever wondered why just about every church service around the world opens with singing, I would say it's because music lets us express our hearts right off the bat. Whatever you've gone through that week, whether joys or sorrows, when you sing to God, it quickly tunes your heart to His presence. There's something powerful behind praise. When you read Scripture, in particular the book of Psalms, you can't help but notice that praise is the anthem of heaven.

> Praise the Lord from the heavens;
>   praise him in the heights above.
> Praise him, all his angels;
>   praise him, all his heavenly hosts.
> Praise him, sun and moon;
>   praise him, all you shining stars.
> Praise him, you highest heavens
>   and you waters above the skies.
> (Ps. 148:1-4)

Many worship leaders I know will often talk about the word

"worship," what it means, how we apply it to our modern-day context. However, "praise" often takes a backseat in the conversation. To be fully equipped as worship leaders, we need to know just as much about praise as we do worship. So, first, what exactly is praise? In the most basic definition, praise is ascribing worth to someone or something. Whenever I tell my kids how great they did on their report card, I'm praising them. Whenever you let your drummer know how awesome he did on that opening groove, you're giving him praise. But as we approach the topic of praise in this chapter, I want to ask you three specific questions:

- Who are you praising?
- How are you praising?
- When are you praising?

The Object of Praise

These questions might be great to go through with your team. They help us get the perspective of praise and to keep the heart of praise at the forefront of our lives. When we live a life of praise throughout our week, we can pour a heart of praise out on Sunday as we lead—or Saturday for you edgy churches. (Secretly we all wish we did Saturday evening church so that we could sleep in on Sundays, but I digress.)

That first question is everything: Who are you praising? Psalm 150 is the very last chapter in the great songbook. The very last verse of that last chapter says this: "Let everything that has breath praise the Lord. Praise the Lord" (Ps. 150:6). That three-word instruction is quite possibly the three words that best sum up the entire book of Psalms. Who do we praise? The Lord. And why do we praise the Lord? We praise God for *who* He is and for *what* He's done.

Do I have any words-of-affirmation people in the house? It's one of my top love languages. Of course, like many guys, my main language is physical touch. I can't walk by my wife without a quick smooch, a shoulder rub, or at the least a "Christian side hug." But if you and I are hanging out and you get a fist bump from me or a high five, it's my way of letting you know we're friends. Words of affirmation rank a close second, and they go a long way with me. For instance, if I show you a song I wrote, yes, I want you to be honest, but start off with the positive. I constantly give out words of affirmation to those around me because I've learned the value of speaking life.

Praise is the way we affirm God with song. It's putting words of affirmation to a melody. Now, often we hear the word "praise" coupled with the word "worship," and there's a reason "praise" and "worship" go together so nicely. But they're not exactly the same thing. As I understand it, here's the basic difference:

- Worship is the way we live our lives expressing God's greatness.
- Praise is the way we physically and verbally demonstrate that worship.

Since praise and affirmation are so closely related, I need to make this caveat. As I said earlier, we can receive praise and give praise. As humans, when we receive affirmation we need to be very careful not to let pride creep in. Pride is the enemy of praise. Pride and praise cannot coexist. One of those two will be the soundtrack of your life.

Are you seeking praise from people or giving praise to Jesus? When you do receive those words of affirmation, what happens? Do you soak it up or offer it up to God's glory? "Fire tests the purity of silver and gold, but a person is tested by being praised" (Prov. 27:21, NLT).

This doesn't mean we can't ever receive a compliment. The question is, are you finding your complete value in that, or do you find your worth in God and therefore your response to every word of affirmation from people is simply gratitude to God?

David wrote in Psalm 145:3, "Great is the LORD and most worthy of praise; his greatness no one can fathom."

God is the only one *most* worthy of praise, and our lives should look like songs lived out in worship. Praise is woven into the fabric of our DNA. Everyone on this planet is praising something or someone. Now the ultimate form of pride is in praising ourselves. That's the moment when we go from gratitude to entitlement. Only God is *most* worthy of our praise. In the *Westminster Shorter Catechism*, one of the most respected books on Christian theology, it says, "Man's chief end is to glorify God and to enjoy Him forever."

Our main purpose in life is to bring Him praise and enjoy His presence.

In the New Testament, we read from the apostle Peter, "But you are a chosen people, a royal priesthood, a holy nation, God's special possession, that you may declare the praises of him who called you out of darkness into his wonderful light" (1 Pet. 2:9).

We were created to declare God's praises. So *who* are you praising?

The Posture of Praise

The next question I want to ask is, *how* are you praising?

I'm a huge YouTube fan. If there's something that I don't know how to do, I head straight to YouTube. I could Google it, but I'm a visual learner, so it helps me to see it. I recently borrowed a pressure washer from a friend to clean off our patio, and for some reason I couldn't get it to start. Sure enough, I did a search for typical problems with this brand of pressure washer and found a video of some random dude fixing the exact problem I was having by taking out a tiny bolt on the bottom and cleaning it. I did what I saw in the video and *voila!* It worked like a charm. I love the Internet!

These days it's easy to look up the how behind anything and get instructions. But you can't learn how to worship on the Internet. When it comes to worship, I think a lot of us are missing the how. We might do what we see being done around us, but do we know *why* we raise our hands in worship? Do we know *how* to express certain types of emotion to God? Just like a teacher utilizes a textbook when teaching their classroom a subject, when it comes to praise and worship, we have a sort of manual that we can go to anytime called the book of Psalms. With 150 chapters, we see different types of songs written in different seasons of life. We see many different viewpoints because very different people wrote it. We also read about the different postures of praise.

Class in Session

Throughout the Bible, the word "praise" appears nearly 250 times. If something appears that many times, we need to pay attention to it, dive into what it means, and learn how we are called to live it out.

In the Hebrew language, seven is known as the number of perfection and completion. Interestingly, there are seven distinct Hebrew words for praise. We're going to go to Hebrew school here for just a moment, so pull out your journal and take some notes. Or you could just use a highlighter.

Here are the seven postures of praise:

1. Halal—to rave, celebrate, to shine, to be clamorously foolish. The best example of this was when David danced before the Lord in 2 Samuel 6, after the Ark of the Covenant was brought back to Israel. He definitely didn't look like a dignified king in that moment, and he could not have cared less. He was partying it up before the King of kings. When was the last time you were willing to look foolish to follow God?

2. Yadah—to throw out your hands, to worship with extended hand. This is where we get our hand-raising posture from.

Psalm 134:2 says, "Lift up your hands in the sanctuary and praise the Lord." Recently at our church in Nashville, during our time of worship I shared that when we raise our hands, it's like a little kid throwing their arms up and saying, "Daddy, pick me up." We're yielding to the God of the universe, and asking Him to hold us in His arms. Hands being raised is a universal sign of surrender. You've seen it in war movies, and you probably did it when you were younger playing dodgeball or paintball. When you lift your arms, it's throwing up that white flag. We're saying, "God, I give up. I've tried it on my own and failed. I need You." I love The Message version of Psalm 63:4: "I bless you every time I take a breath; My arms wave like banners of praise to you."

I've heard my friend Michael Farren say, "Your heart sometimes follows your hands." If you are having a hard time surrendering to God, take this posture of humility.

3. Towdah—to extend your hands in adoration, avowal, or acceptance. Often with Thanksgiving.

Psalm 107:22 says, "Let them offer sacrifices of thanksgiving and sing joyfully about his glorious acts" (NLT). There's a beautiful way that the Quakers have prayed for hundreds of years that demonstrates this type of praise. With their palms facing upward, they ask God to pour out His blessing, as they take a posture of receptivity. Then they turn their palms downward to the ground and pray that everything they need to let go of would be released. Prayer and praise go hand in hand!

4. Shabach—to shout, to address in a loud tone, to triumph! Psalm 47:1 says, "Come, everyone! Clap your hands! Shout to God with joyful praise!" (NLT). There are times when we whisper and times when we need to shout. I remember leading worship at a summer camp, and you could sense a spirit of heaviness the entire week. During one of our times of worship, I felt impressed by the Spirit to talk about this Shabach praise. We were going into the Hillsong classic "Shout Unto God." I didn't want us to just casually sing those lyrics. So right in the middle of the song I counted to three and we all let out a massive shout of praise. You could literally feel the oppression breaking, as a shout of victory went out. I think we may have even broken a window or two!

5. Barak—to kneel down, to bless God as an act of adoration.

Psalm 95:6 says, "Come, let us worship and bow down. Let us kneel before the LORD our maker" (NLT). Here yet again, you can see how praise and prayer often take the same posture. Bowing is a posture of submission and humility. We can't worship a God that we're not humble before. I know that many of our current worship environments don't have the greatest seating arrangements to bow, but there is something beautiful that happens when we do. Find times to get in this position during your prayer times at home. Encourage your team to do this in their prayer lives too!

6. Zamar—to pluck the strings of an instrument, to sing, accompanied with music. For every guitar player reading, this is probably your favorite way to praise.

Psalm 57:7 says, "My heart, O God, is steadfast, my heart is steadfast; I will sing and make music." Aldous Huxley said, "After silence, that which comes nearest to expressing the inexpressible is music." Songs have always filled people with emotion. If you have a gift to play, use it to praise!

7. Tehillah—singing halal, or praise; using your voice to sing hymns of the Spirit.

Here's the vocal side of musical instruments. It's important to note that although these are Hebrew words, these seven forms of praise weren't just in the Old Testament. You can see nearly all seven demonstrated throughout the New Testament as well. These forms of praise are for the Church today! The nice thing about singing is that you can do it anywhere, anytime. Whether you're a car-radio praiser or a shower-only praiser, use your voice to declare God's goodness!

Through these seven different words for praise, we can see many different ways to verbally and physically honor God. We have a diverse portfolio of expression, each holding a different emotion. When we take a posture of praise and humility, God meets us with His power and presence.

The Catapult

The incredible thing about praise is that not only do we enter God's presence by praising—"I will enter his gates with Thanksgiving in my heart, enter his courts with praise" (Ps. 100:4)—but God also enters *our* presence through praise: "Yet You are holy, enthroned on the praises of Israel" (Ps. 22:3). It's a two-way street. God comes into our midst when we praise, and we are welcomed into His presence through praises of thanksgiving. I'm reminded of Matt Redman's song "Here for You," as the first line sings, "Let our praise be your welcome, let our songs be a sign, we are here for You."

I know that however many people are reading this, each one of you has a very unique story, experience, and church background. Some of us may come from a highly expressive upbringing, in our home life and in our church life. Others not so much. When I first started dating Sarah, I brought her to my dad's church. We were a nondenominational church that was not afraid of getting our expressive praise on. I'll admit, sometimes it got a little crazy. Nowadays I consider myself a Pentecostal with a seatbelt on, but back then you never knew what Sunday was going to look like!

Sarah came from a more conservative and liturgical background, where they didn't dance or raise their hands in service, yet they sang very loudly, and with passion. It was during a time we were both singing the song "Freedom Reigns" by Rita Springer that something clicked for her and she raised her hands in worship. That was a breakthrough moment when she was able to tie together Scripture and song, and raising hands began to make sense in worship for her. It brought a new freedom in her walk with Jesus, and now it's just second nature during worship. I know we're all created uniquely and that we each have a unique way to worship. As Mark Batterson says, "No one can worship God like you, or for you!"

There are many different ways to worship, different styles of song, dance, music, and that is part of the freedom that comes by the Spirit of God in worship. Yet I also believe there are ways to worship that the Bible not only encourages us to do but also instructs us to do in order to bless the Lord and to walk in blessing, as we've just seen throughout the book of Psalms.

A while ago, a friend of mine was having a really hard time expressing praise to God in church. He would stand pretty stoically, usually arms crossed, and just barely sing under his breath. He said it wasn't his style. However, this same guy was like Richard Simmons if you got him in front of an NFL game! He'd be jumping up and down, yelling at the top of his lungs, whenever his team got a first down. Many of us can relate, and it doesn't just apply to sports fans. We can cheer for our favorite teams, scream at concerts with our favorite bands, paint our faces, throw Super Bowl parties; but when we come to church, do we even realize the celebration that we get to take part in? Church is supposed to be a party! At Bridges Nashville, I tell our congregation that this is a sacred celebration. It's rock 'n roll meets reverence.

I want to challenge you to let the Psalms be a guideline to how you worship, how you live out praise to Jesus, and especially how you lead others in worship. I often get this question from worship leaders: "Why is my church so expressionless during our service?" Help people connect the dots and see how our physical posture is tied to our verbal praise. I think these seven Hebrew words for praise can help connect people to new ways of expression!

At All Times

Here's the last question I'll ask in this chapter: *When* are you praising?

Psalm 34:1 says, "I will praise the LORD at all times. I will constantly speak his praises" (NLT). There are a lot of times when praising God is the *last* thing on my mind. As worship leaders and worship teams, it can be very easy to get into a routine, where the only time we are praising is when we're scheduled to. Rehearsals and services can throw us into a "professional praise" mindset. You've heard it before: you can't lead people on a Sunday where you haven't been all week. Praise isn't just a "church" thing; it's an all-day, all-week thing! It's how we live a life of worship!

The reality is that some of us are running on empty. We're often pouring out more than we're putting in. We don't get enough sleep, we stay up too late, and our lives are so busy. But we have to make God's presence a priority. Even when I'm drained at the end of a long work-day, I've found that my strength is renewed in the Lord when I give the very last ounce of my energy in praise. I can promise you that God will give you fresh energy when you give yours to Him. Worship Him in the quiet place of your home, and wait on Him in His presence. We read in Isaiah 40:31, ". . . but those who hope in the LORD will renew their strength. They will soar on wings like eagles; they will run and not grow weary, they will walk and not be faint." Praise Him when you've got nothing left to give and watch how God will give you the extra measure of strength that you need!

Praising the Lord at all times also means to praise in the hard times. I call it "worship through hardship." When we choose to walk by faith and not by sight, we can sing a song of praise even when it doesn't look like the promise. If you praise in the *process*, you'll praise in the *promise*.

You see, praise is a mindset. Praise is not a natural reaction; it's an intentional response. Don't be moved by what you see but by *who* you know. That will lead you to praise even when it doesn't make sense around you.

Make the choice to bless the Lord at all times. If you want a good example of when praise happened in the midst of chaos, go to the ancient kings of Judah. This story shows us that a breakthrough often happens right before the breakdown.

In 2 Chronicles 20, we read about Jehoshaphat's army. There were many kings in the Old Testament who did evil in the sight of the Lord. But Jehoshaphat was a rare breed who did what was *right* in the sight of the Lord. He followed in the ways of David. He found his strength in God and not in his own power. In this particular passage, three armies were attacking Judah. Things looked grim. So the king did what anyone would do as thousands of soldiers marched upon his home; he worshiped! As he did, the prophet spoke, giving him this encourage-ment: "Do not be discouraged for the battle isn't yours. It belongs to the Lord." Come on, somebody! Then it says this:

> After consulting the people, Jehoshaphat appointed men to sing to the Lord and to praise him for the splendor of his holiness as they went out at the head of the army, saying: "Give thanks

to the Lord, for his love endures forever." As they began to sing and praise, the Lord set ambushes against the men of Ammon and Moab and Mount Seir who were invading Judah, and they were defeated.

He had his worship team lead the fight. That's like the president calling up some of the most popular rock bands of our time and saying, "Hey, we're about to go into war. Could you guys go up ahead of the tanks and helicopters and start rocking out?" It probably looked like a crazy move, and it was. Crazy awesome! Because as they sang praises to God, the Lord set an ambush on the enemy and took care of the entire fleet. Scripture tells us that "not one man was left standing."

Praise in the hard times and press in to God's presence. When you're faced with hardship, don't let your heart fail. Never let your current circumstance dictate how you worship God, because He's always worthy. The story of Jehoshaphat tells us that when we focus on our heavenly Father, over our earthly circumstances, the battle is won. Praise lets us focus on our eternal identity instead of on our worldly problems. It's not about just forgetting our reality; it's about entrusting it into the hands of a God who does the impossible. When we give God praise in the hard times, it sends a threefold message: first, to the enemy that he's been defeated; second, to God that we trust in Him, even in the midst of a battle; third, to our own hearts that we won't be shaken by our surroundings. Don't let fear outweigh your faith.

Of course, the other side of the coin is praising God when everything is going smoothly. When life is working like we want it to, many times it's easy to forget to praise God because we feel like we've got it. Yet, just as much as Psalm 34 is about praising God in the hard times, it also includes the good times, because it says, "I will praise the Lord at *all* times." When the seas of life are calm, it's easy to let pride seep in, and as we said earlier, pride and praise cannot coexist. There's an old Hebrew saying: whatever you don't thank God for, it's as if you're stealing a blessing. Whatever you don't turn into praise becomes pride!

We must always know where blessing comes from. We must teach our churches to look to God in every season, to know where our help comes from. "I lift up my eyes to the mountains—where does my help come from? My help comes from the Lord, the Maker of heaven and earth" (Ps. 121:1-2). Praise is what we were created for—in the good times, the hard times, and everything in between. If you're reading these pages, you have a reason to praise. Why? Because you have breath in your lungs. "Let everything that has breath praise the Lord."

Praise God for who He is.

Praise God for what He's done.

Praise God for what's to come. Amen.

Closing Thought

"Praise" is a word often heard in church. Some common phrases used are "Praise the Lord!" or "God is worthy to be praised!" If you've been in church any amount of time, you've probably heard these or similar exhortations. But what does it really mean to praise the Lord? In Psalm 150:1-6, the Bible says:

> Praise the Lord.
> Praise God in his sanctuary;
> praise him in his mighty heavens.
> Praise him for his acts of power;
> praise him for his surpassing greatness.
> Praise him with the sounding of the trumpet,
> praise him with the harp and lyre,
> praise him with timbrel and dancing,
> praise him with the strings and pipe,
> praise him with the clash of cymbals,
> praise him with resounding cymbals.
> Let everything that has breath praise the Lord.
> Praise the Lord.

The Hebrew word for "praise" in this passage means "to boast," "to make a fool of," or "to act madly." It reminds me of David in 2 Samuel 6. He danced before the Lord and praised God so wildly that he apparently danced out of his clothes! Saul's daughter scolded him for acting so "undistinguished." But David said he'd gladly make a fool of himself and act even more "undignified" in order to praise God! Praise is not limited to singing, dancing, or playing songs to God. Praise should be part of our lifestyle! When we honor God's temple, which is our bodies, by prioritizing our health and well-being, we're praising God! When we boast about

His goodness to others and put the spotlight on Jesus in our daily lives, we're praising God! And it's that type of praise that has the power to shift things in our favor and give us victory over circumstances we face. I encourage you to make praise your daily posture and watch it transform your life!

Jemia Wingard
Recording artist, speaker, and songwriter

CHAPTER 8

Authenticity

In 1988, German record producer Frank Farian discovered a couple of aspiring young models, Rob Pilatus and Fabrice Morvan. He quickly went into the studio and created a dance pop album that would take the music world by storm. Armed with incredible dance moves, stunning drum beats, and the *original* "Blue Steel" model stare, Milli Vanilli soon became a household name. They gave us several chart topping '80s classics, including "Blame It on the Rain" and "Girl, You Know It's True." This dynamic duo went on to sell nearly 30 million singles, packed arenas on their world tours, and even took home the Grammy for "Best New Artist" in 1990.

Their success was short-lived, however, when a live concert on MTV (in front of millions of adoring fans) revealed that the group had been lip-syncing the entire time. The backing track, played from backstage, got caught on a loop—"Girl you know . . . girl you know . . . girl you know"—and the scam was publicly exposed. Rob and Fab raced offstage, and over the next few years, the band lost the record deal, lost the fans, and became the first act to ever be stripped of a Grammy. Rob and Fab tried to make it back to the top and released an album using their own voices, with their own songs, under their own names. But just imagine "Zoolander" meets karaoke. Their new album barely sold 2,000 copies, and the group soon faded into musical oblivion. Their secret was out, and apparently the world doesn't like fake.

I pretty much watch only two types of TV: sports and reality shows.

It's something I'm praying through, and for my wife's sake, I'd ask for your prayers. One of my favorite shows centers around a pawn shop where people come in with items they believe to be valuable, mostly antiques; some memorabilia is even autographed. The owners of the shop then call up an authenticator to come and put it under the microscope, to check its authenticity and assess its value. In one episode a lady brought in an old acoustic guitar. The antique guitar on its own would have been considered highly valuable simply due to its age, but there were four signatures on it that could have significantly upped the ante: John, Paul, George, and Ringo. That's right, the Beatles had all four signed this instrument, or so she claimed. After calling down the authenticator to verify the Fab Four's penmanship, sadly it turned out she had been fooled by a forgery. Had those signatures been real, the guitar would have been valued around $100,000. However, not only was it not given that high price tag, but the antique guitar, also a treasure, was now deemed worthless because of the four fake autographs on it. The value was stripped by inauthenticity.

You may be starting to catch where I'm going with this. In Luke 8:17, we see a picture of the Great Authenticator: "For all that is secret will eventually be brought into the open, and everything that is concealed will be brought to light and made know to all."

A 2014 study by Cohn & Wolfe revealed that the number-one thing consumers look for in a brand they support isn't innovation or a low price point; it's authenticity. Here's the key: God's interested in the same thing. "Authentic" is simply defined as "real, genuine, and true." In John 4:23, Jesus tells us, "Yet a time is coming and *has now come* when the true worshipers will worship the Father in the Spirit and in truth, for they are the kind of worshipers the Father seeks." God is after authentic worship, and He deserves nothing less. He can always sniff out the true from the fake. The Greek word for "truth" in this passage is *aletheia*. It's the same word that Jesus uses to describe Himself in John 14:6, when He says, "I am the way, the truth, and the life." It's a word that signifies evidence, as in a court case. The truth, as in a case, will always set you free and reveals the authenticity of the matter. There are 109 instances of this word for truth in the New Testament. It's something Jesus displays, and it's something He wants to see in us.

What Jesus is saying in Luke 8 and John 4 is this: you cannot live a double life. Who you are when no one is watching will always shape who you are when everyone is watching.

Now, Jesus said these words in a culture that was rampant with false gods and idols. Pagan Rome alone had a dozen gods and goddesses at the core of their worship. (Strange side note: most of our planets are named after them.) Every culture in that day and age had objects of worship; and then there were those who claimed to be living for the one true God, Yahweh, and were doing so just on the outside. Pharisees and Sadducees were a couple of the leading religious classes, and today we read often of their hypocrisy. It's easy for us to read about these people and not realize we're often guilty of the same exact crime—putting on a show while the heart is on a different page. In Matthew 23, Jesus calls this type of people "whitewashed tombs":

> Woe to you, teachers of the law and Pharisees, you hypocrites! You are like whitewashed tombs, which look beautiful on the outside but on the inside are full of the bones of the dead and everything unclean. In the same way, on the outside you appear to people as righteous but on the inside you are full of hypocrisy and wickedness. (vv. 27-28)

Pretty on the outside, dead on the inside. I got a lesson on "white-washing" from my dad, whose first job was as a dairy hand at a farm in Pennsylvania. He said that when cows get together, they make quite a mess, on everything. A lot of their waste ends up on the walls, and to help the barn not look like a "house of poo," they'd simply paint over it every now and again with white paint. Pretty disgusting when you think about it. It's not bad to look at, but when you investigate and go beneath the surface, it starts to stink. Literally.

The fact is, our world is desperate for authenticity, something real. And yet everywhere we look, we see the alternative. It seems like nearly every week a new political scandal comes to light, an athlete whom we all admire is found to be taking steroids, and sadly, even in the Church, we've seen fellow pastors and worship leaders make the headlines for not the greatest reasons. As worshipers and Christ-followers, we have to set the mark for what a true lifestyle is meant to look like.

But it's not easy, is it?

Twitter, Instagram, Facebook, Snapchat, and for all you kids out there, TikTok—these are some of the leading social media platforms.

I'm sure by the time this book is released there will be a couple of new sites. The Internet helps us create our own world, and we post what we want the world to think about us. We present our image in the best possible light, through the best filters. We don't post the mundane, because who wants that? We don't share the peanut butter and jelly sandwiches; we share the Ruth's Chris steak dinner. We don't share a morning-breath-induced, fresh-out-of-bed selfie; we share the outfit that's ready for a night out on the town. We don't share the worship team in a rehearsal working through chord charts; we share the stage shot with all the lights and fog machines and hundreds of hands lifted high. We want everyone to think that we've got it all together, while on the inside we might be going through a battlefield. I wonder if all of the images that we're sharing are a true reflection of our hearts. Or would we show our highlight reel to Jesus only to hear, "These people honor me with their lips, but their hearts are far from me" (Matt. 15:8). Lip service. Lip-syncing.

To be worship leaders, teams, and pastors who honor God with our hearts, we need to live with authenticity. We can't take our teams where we haven't been personally. We can't lead our churches to the secret place of God's presence if we don't know the way.

What Is Worship

So, how do we live out a life of authentic worship? I think first we need to expand our view of what worship is! The answer lies in the Hebrew word for "worship": *avodah*, which means "daily living." It comes from Paul's words in Romans 12:1: "Therefore, I urge you, brothers and sisters, in view of God's mercy, to offer your bodies as a living sacrifice, holy and pleasing to God—this is your true and proper worship."

Worship in the original Greek has little to do with a song set we sing on a Sunday morning; it's the life we live in the day to day. I'm sure you've heard that somewhere down the line, but I don't want you to discredit the beautiful tie-in with music. There's a reason we call our song offering to God "worship." You see, the reason musical worship is so powerful is that in most cultures, song is the easiest and most authentic way to express your heart. Sometimes we can only *sing* what we want to say to God. With a song, you can tell God where your heart is. You can sing your prayers.

Worship is emotional and intellectual. In fact, I believe there's a revelation in John 4, when Jesus tells us to worship God in "spirit and truth." I see a correlation for "spirit and truth" to be "heart and mind." Worship is both emotional and intellectual. God wants you to *feel* Him and to *know* Him. It's the head *and* the heart. God knows the power of music and its ability to morph those two worlds of mind and heart together. All of heaven is filled with the sound of worship, and any time we truly engage in that eternal force, it brings a little heaven to Earth. When we worship here on Earth, we are a mirror image of what happens around the throne night and day.

But it can't just happen on Sundays. Worship is our "daily living," and you don't just breathe one day a week, just like you wouldn't eat one meal a day. And I certainly wouldn't tell my wife I love her for only an hour on the weekend.

You see, it's the six days and 20-something hours outside of a church service that make worship authentic. The songs we sing and lead every weekend are not the end all and be all but rather the verbal declaration and physical expression of our heart's position. I like to think of our church service as a time when the people of God get together to sing of God's past faithfulness and to prophecy in song of His future faithfulness. We've seen God move, and we know He'll do it again. Songs become altars, and our corporate worship is like an anthem of hope, infusing the body of Christ with faith. And for those in our midst who may not yet have a relationship with God, they're seeing what that looks like! Worship can be the most authentic moment of your life, because it's where the veil is lifted and total transparency is needed. It's where you pour your heart out to your Dad.

To be honest, I used to read this Luke 8 verse specifically through the lens of sin, and think to myself, *If I'm doing my own thing and not walking with God in my private life, then that will eventually be exposed in the open.* If I'm cussing in the car at traffic, lashing out in anger at home, feeding my soul with carnal and flesh-driven desire, then that will eventually come out in my workplace and in public. And that's true, but it's also true about how we worship. The private-to-public transfer also works the other way. If I'm singing songs to God when I don't have a microphone in front of me; if I'm reading His Word throughout the week when I don't have to prepare a message; if I'm loving my family and serving my neighbors, then all those will naturally pour out when I'm surrounded by the Church. How you worship privately sets the tone for authentic worship publicly. There's no switch-flipping necessary for when you step onto a stage to lead worship. It's not "go time"; it's "I've been here all week and this is just another moment in God's presence." The only difference is that you get to lead others into that space. What a privilege!

Worshiping in spirit and truth causes one to set their eyes on Jesus, and as the old hymn suggests, the things of this world will grow strangely dim. We need a church filled with worship that is straight from the heart—messy, broken, and true. God wants to hear the song of our hearts, not just a manufactured script. I think this is why it's so important to allow for space and silence in our worship times. If the only song we let people sing is the words we put up on a screen, I'm afraid it's like me only telling my wife I love her with a Hallmark card I bought from the store. Yes, it's important to help people sing their worship. In fact, sometimes we need to teach that. However, there comes a point when people get to an intimacy with God and they can sing their own song. That's a win.

As I said earlier, I love reality TV. It's amazing because it's real and raw (or supposed to be at least), and it tells the story of humanity. Nothing will make me tune out of a show faster than when it claims to be reality but you can clearly tell it's scripted. It loses the genuineness, and most times it loses the conflict. See, it's the conflict in our real-life struggles that makes it authentic. God isn't afraid of your conflict, your battles, or your tension. Don't put on your church face and appear to be put together. It's okay to not be okay. His strength is made perfect in our weakness. If we have it all put together and present our lives through an Instagram filter, then we are masking the truth and hiding the battles that we're not meant to fight alone. People always identify with struggles over success, and with those who are real, over those who look like they have it all together. So be real with God, with yourself, and with others.

Don't Leak

There's a very important side of leadership that I have to address at this point. While we have the absolute desire to lead authentically, we cannot lead effectively if we're wounded. We *can* lead with a limp; that's just the proof that we've been through some stuff and have come out on the other side stronger. I heard Steven Furtick preach a message once about leading from your scars and not your wounds. Leading from your scars shows that God heals and has brought you through a season. Leading from your wounds shows that you're still trying to fight on your own, and you'll usually bleed all over the ones you're called to lead. Sorry if that was a little graphic, but hey, we're talking rawness here.

Sometimes, when you're going through a mess, and you know that God is doing soul work on you, you might need to step down for a season so that you can become whole. There's authenticity in seeing a leader who is completely burned out take a break. It only further speaks to the truth of who we are as human. Your team will respect you, and your church will see a testimony. I'm always inspired when I see a pastor take an extended sabbatical. It speaks to their security, their strength, and their dependence on God. If you're in that season right now, where you need to take a break, talk with your pastor. If you're in a broken and hurting season, come to the Father as a son or daughter, not as a worship leader. If you're in a place where you know you can't lead worship and mean what you sing, you might need to step down.

In his book *Lost and Found*, Ed Stetzer writes that it's a lack of transparency in leadership that has turned many of today's generation away from the Church. If we want to lead others in authenticity, we need to be real. Leadership transparency is influencing others to change and make an impact by allowing the light to pass through who we are. But there's a side to authenticity that we haven't yet talked about and it's vital when it comes to leadership.

It's About Identity

David went down as the greatest king in ancient Israel largely because from an early age he knew his identity. He knew who he was, and he knew *whose* he was. Identity always leads to authenticity. At this moment in the history of the world, and all throughout our culture, we have an identity crisis. It seems like the topic of authenticity has never been more at the forefront, but the example of it has never been more in the backdrop.

As worship leaders, pastors, and servants, we must know our identity. Everything else we do will stem from a proper understanding of who we are. When we know our identity, we can live our truest lives. And when we know our eternal calling, we become our most effective earthly versions.

Back to David. He was authentic and transparent, for better or for worse. He was always real, even when it got him into trouble. Long before David was king in a palace, he worshiped in the pastures. He wrote songs as a kid, and that heart of worship carried him to a ripe old age. Even as a teenager in his most glorious rumble, he had to be his true self to defeat Goliath.

Let me set the stage. Israel is at war with the Philistines, and there's a giant, a mountain of a man if you will. Goliath stands 9 feet tall, and he's taunting the army of Israel night and day, telling them to send out a man to fight him, *mano a mano*. Whichever nation's champion won, that nation would be the victor. David, just a teenager at this point, is rocking some Uber Eats and brings his brothers a meal on the battle-field. That's when he catches wind of what's happening in the fight.

> David said to Saul, "Let no one lose heart on account of this Philistine; your servant will go and fight him." Saul replied, "You are not able to go out against this Philistine and fight him; you are only a young man, and he has been a warrior from his youth." . . . Then Saul dressed David in his own tunic. He put a coat of armor on him and a bronze helmet on his head. David fastened on his sword over the tunic and tried walking around, because he was not used to them. "I cannot go in these," he said to Saul, "because I am not used to them." So he took them off. Then he took his staff in his hand, chose five smooth stones from the stream, put them in the pouch of his shepherd's bag and, with his sling in his hand, approached the Philistine. (1 Sam. 17:33-34, 38-40)

We know the story: David takes down Goliath, becomes a hero, and starts a long journey to the throne (preceded by many years of living like a fugitive). What made David so unique among all the kings of Israel was that he was confident in his identity. He was a man after God's own heart. In this passage, Saul tried to put his identity on David by dressing David in his tunic and armor. He was telling young David, "Here's how I do it, and here's how it's been done." But that wasn't David's bag. Don't let other people's expectations define you. If it doesn't line up with God's Word and if it doesn't resonate in your spirit as you pray, then you might need to toss it to the side. I love how Mark Batterson talks about criticism: "Don't let an arrow of criticism pierce your heart, unless it first passes through the filter of Scripture."

You see, in the previous chapter, before this colossal showdown, the prophet Samuel showed up to anoint David. Any one of David's older brothers would have been given the nod because of their outward looks. But the prophet wasn't after a white-washed tomb. He was looking for someone who could lead the nation in the ways of God. The Lord does not look at the things people look at. People look at the outward appearance, but the Lord looks at the heart (see 1 Sam. 16:7).

Samuel saw something special in the young shepherd boy and spoke identity over him as the future king. Samuel told David who he was through God's eyes, whereas Saul told David who he was through man's eyes. David's confidence was in being a child of God. That's why he told Goliath, "I come to you in the name of the Lord." That phrase "in the name" is an identity marker. David found who he was in the pasture as a shepherd long before he made it to the palace as a king. So many people in his journey tried putting their agenda and expectations on him, but his confidence was in the God who called him before he had any friends or fans.

In a sense, Saul was trying to put his label on David, not just his armor. Maybe he even wanted the soldiers who were watching from a distance to see his armor in action on the battlefield and believe that their cowardly king had suddenly gotten the guts to take on the giant. But David wouldn't take the bait. He went with nothing but the name of the Lord, a sling, and some stones. To most of those trained soldiers' eyes, it probably looked like a suicide mission, yet David actually had the advantage in the fight because he knew who he was and what he was called to. Better yet, he knew who his Father was and that He had his back. And all throughout David's life, he kept realigning his heart to God. He never had to push his position or power. When you put God first, opportunities seem to find you.

No Need to Prove

God calls us valued whether or not we do anything to prove it. We're loved from the beginning. Think about this: before Jesus did any miracles, before He taught a single sermon, and long before the cross, God shouted out to the world how much He loved His Son: "And a voice from heaven said, 'This is my Son, whom I love; with him I am well pleased'" (Matt. 3:17).

God loves you, not for what you can do, but simply because you're His child. When you say yes to following Jesus, you become in Christ. That's your identity. When you have your identity down, you'll lead with authenticity, and you'll help others discover their path. Here are a few key verses that reveal identity:

- 2 Corinthians 5:17—"If anyone is in Christ they are a new creation."
- Ephesians 2:10—"For we are God's masterpiece. He has created us anew in Christ Jesus, so we can do the good things he planned for us long ago."
- 1 Peter 2:9—"But you are not like that, for you are a chosen people. You are royal priests, a holy nation, God's very own possession. As a result, you can show others the goodness of God, for he called you out of the darkness into his wonderful light."

If you're looking to know who you are as a Christ follower, check out Romans 8. It's my favorite chapter in the entire Bible because it reveals so much about who we are. It's like the driver's license of a Christian. When you know who you are, you don't need to measure up to others.

Confidence Over Comparison

One of the biggest things stealing the identity of worship leaders everywhere is the comparison game. By default, when we start living by comparison, trying to measure up to other people and false expectations, we lose ourselves, and authenticity goes out the window. It's so easy to get lost on social media—seeing how everyone else is doing it, how big their church is, how amazing their stage production is, how many musicians they have in their worship band rotation—and let the comparison game undermine your role and the assignment God has placed you in. One of the most powerful messages I've ever heard on the topic of worship was from Jesse Reeves at Austin Stone Worship Conference. He likened the overload of worship highlight reels to pornography. If you find yourself belittling your ministry by lusting after the big stage and huge crowds that you see in someone else's ministry, then you're missing it.

Even with the churches that are doing ministry on a huge scale and the leaders with enormous platforms, a picture doesn't tell the whole story. Many of them have spent decades in the shadows, working on the small things, being faithful with little, and God has given them more because He knows what they can do and where their heart is. I've had the opportunity to work alongside some incredible leaders in the faith who have a lot of influence. I can honestly say, from my view, that God blesses what He sees as authentic. In these cases, there was a lot of blood, sweat, and tears before there was any influence. And funny enough, most people who end up with a large following never asked for it. If you want the following of others more than you want to follow Jesus, you'll self-destruct. Either you'll get the following only to see that it's not all it's cracked up to be, or you'll never be given influence, because just like Samuel said, "God looks at the heart." So don't let the comparison game discredit what God is doing in your season! You can't compare apples to oranges. What is successful in the kingdom has nothing to do with what is successful in the world. Faithfulness, obedience, and a life that shows Jesus and leads others to Him show success. Comparison is an identity thief.

Another "King" Story

Born in 1935 in Tupelo, Mississippi, Elvis Presley rose from humble beginnings to the highest fame. He sold more than a billion albums and still holds the record for most hit singles on the U.S. charts and most number-one albums by a male solo artist. He was a rock star and a movie star. While his much-debated death in 1977 shocked the world, it came as no surprise that dozens, and soon hundreds, of Elvis impersonators stepped up to try to become the next king of rock 'n roll. One of the most talented entertainers was Jimmy "Orion" Ellis. In fact, it was a widespread rumor that Orion was Elvis come back from the dead. His true identity was shielded from the public by his signature look, a mask over his face, which only added to the mystery. His voice was nearly identical to Elvis. Orion was so talented that he signed a record deal with Sun Records, the same label Elvis, Johnny Cash, and Jerry Lee Lewis had been signed to right here in Nashville.

Many people felt that Orion's voice was actually sweeter than Elvis's. In the documentary *Orion: The Man Who Would Be King*, music critics wondered that if Orion had never worn the mask and had come out on his own talent, would he have been an artist just as popular, if not even more so, than Elvis. During a concert in 1983, he tore off his mask, vowing to never wear it again. Sadly, his popularity completely dwindled because he had built his entire career off of being compared to Elvis Presley instead of on his confidence in his own identity.

The King of Kings

Jesus was constantly rewiring His followers to open their eyes to their true identity. In many of His messages, He used the phrase "you have heard it said . . . but I tell you." He often spoke about the new covenant. Most of His parables were about the kingdom of heaven. He pointed to the outpouring of the Holy Spirit. He was all about speaking new life into people. One of the things that people back then—and also people for the last 2,000 years—got hung up on was comparison. Something inside us naturally defaults to finding our value and worth by the actions and words of other people. In Luke 9 we see the comparison game breaking out among the disciples:

> An argument started among the disciples as to which of them would be the greatest. Jesus, knowing their thoughts, took a little child and had him stand beside him. Then he said to them, "Whoever welcomes this little child in my name welcomes me; and whoever welcomes me welcomes the one who sent me. For it is the one who is least among you all who is the greatest." "Master," said John, "we saw someone driving out demons in your name and we tried to stop him, because he is not one of us." "Do not stop him," Jesus said, "for whoever is not against you is for you." (vv. 46-50)

In this passage, the disciples first try to match up against each other, and then they try to match up against those outside the 12—other followers who were operating in the name of Jesus. There might have been a little pride here creeping in. "We're the dudes who roll with Jesus; we're the only ones who can do that kind of stuff. Who are these chumps?" But Jesus squashes it by telling them that if you want to be great in the Kingdom, you have to humble yourself. He didn't have time to waste sizing up against another. Jesus knew that competing and comparing yourself to anyone or anything is sideways energy.

Comparison Kills Contentment

If your identity isn't in Christ, then it becomes rooted in competing with others. You can't compare your strengths to someone else's weaknesses. Likewise, don't compare your weaknesses to someone else's strengths. That's when you either start to think you're *better* than you are, which is self-righteousness, or you start to feel insecure and worthless, which is self-loathing.

There are lies that say, "I'm not good enough," "I have nothing to offer," "God could never use someone like me to do great things." When we live by comparison, we focus on our weaknesses, how we fall short, instead of how we add up.

I know firsthand how comparison kills contentment, from my early days living in Nashville. Sarah and I first moved to Music City in 2005 when I signed a publishing deal out of college. I was so focused on winning a Grammy and trying to land songs on the biggest records that whenever I had a success in my songwriting, it wasn't good enough. When I got a song on the radio, it was just okay. I had a song hit the Billboard 20 in Gospel, but it wasn't number one, so it wasn't good enough. When I got a song placed on a commercial, it wasn't bringing in the payday that my friend's song did, so it wasn't good enough. I knew other writers in town who were less experienced than I was and yet were writing better songs, making more money, and steadily climbing up the songwriter ladder in Nashville. I was so focused on *what* they were doing that I was missing the very joy in *my* story. There is a healthy type of comparison when it drives you to work hard and live with passion, but I'm talking about an unhealthy comparison that destroys your joy.

Comparison Creates Confusion

We all have a unique calling from God. We've all been wired and created for a purpose. Someone once told me that purpose is like a key. We've all been given a key that unlocks something here on Earth, that only we can open. Don't lose your key. Don't get your assignment confused with someone else's journey. If you're called to do something, don't compare that with those who may have a more public or prominent assignment. We need pastors in rural towns just as much as in large cities. We need worship leaders in the suburban megachurch just as much as we need them in the centuries-old farm church. It takes all kinds.

Comparison always leads to envy and jealousy, two qualities God is not after. You will miss what God is speaking in your season when you're too busy looking at someone else's assignment. Donald Clifton, the man behind *StrengthsFinders*, defined social comparison: it's where we find value in how we stack up against others. We see ourselves for what we are *not* instead of who we *are!* Paul warned the early church against this.

> The human body has many parts, but the many parts make up one whole body. So it is with the body of Christ. Some of us are Jews, some are Gentiles, some are slaves, and some are free. But we have all been baptized into one body by one Spirit, and we all share the same Spirit. Yes, the body has many different parts, not just one part. If the foot says, "I am not a part of the body because I am not a hand," that does not make it any less a part of the body. And if the ear says, "I am not part of the body because I am not an eye," would that make it any less a part of the body? If the whole body were an eye, how would you hear? Or if your whole body were an ear, how would you smell anything? But our bodies have many parts, and God has put each part just where he wants it. (1 Cor. 12:12-18)

Inputs and Outcomes

We are all a unique part of the body of Christ. Here's the point: we are *all* called by the same God. As Christians, we're all part of His Church. Whether you're leading a flock of 25 sheep or 2,500, I can guarantee that God looks at the motives and condition of the heart and not the size or statistics of the ministry. He doesn't value one church or platform over the other, just like a parent wouldn't have a favorite kid (or shouldn't have a favorite kid). So many times we get caught up in the outcomes and results of our ministries, when those are really up to God. What you and I can control are the inputs. What will you do to go deeper, and will you respond to the call in obedience? You put *in* the obedience and let God get *out* what He desires. We can't get lost in comparison.

If you're a finger in the body of Christ, don't compare yourself to an ear. It doesn't make sense. You might be an AC joint. You can't see the joint but, man, when that thing gets injured, you can hardly operate.

Some years ago I was leading worship at a youth camp, and the kids all dared me to go down the half-pipe on a skateboard. And I did what any sensible adult would do: I took the dare. Let's just say skateboard 1, Kurtis 0. There's a video out there if you want to see it, but it was a pretty rough spill. I tore my AC joint in my shoulder and had to lead worship playing piano one-handed for the rest of the camp.

That episode taught me that just because you can't see something in the body doesn't make it less important. Some of us might not be in a highly visible role, but *visibility doesn't determine value.* Think about it from a musician's perspective. It doesn't matter how incredible the band is; if you have someone on the soundboard who doesn't know what they're doing, it's going to sound bad in the house! The mix engineer is usually an unseen role, and yet they are often the MVP when it comes to a great sound. For all the behind-the-scenes A/V team people reading this, you folks are my heroes!

Every part of the body is needed. And it shouldn't ever be about us when we're pointing to Him! He is the goal, the prize, the one we should set our eyes on. Let your confidence come in who He says you are.

When I was 11 years old, my dad spoke a word over me that I would one day be a worship leader. He didn't compare me to anyone or tell me to be the next Hillsong. He didn't want me to be the next anybody; he just wanted me to be the best Kurtis. He said I had what it took, and even if I became the worst musician of all time, I'd still be his son. And that was what gave me the confidence to be all I could be.

Your heavenly father is saying "I love you," "You've got it," and "You're my kid." That's how we go from comparison to confidence— because of who we are in Christ, and because of *whose* we are!

Worship is a front door into God's presence. And His presence is the place where identity, authenticity, transparency, and vulnerability win out. God's presence is a place of intimacy. It's where all the masks are stripped away. You can't have authentic worship without vulnerability. As I've shared in this chapter, worship is where our hearts are exposed. It's where surrender and spirit collide.

Worship in the quiet places of your life, when no one else is around, without a microphone or a team to lead. Worship God just to be with Him. To be a true worship leader you have to sometimes lead yourself in worship before you can lead a congregation. If the only time you sing to Jesus is when you have a mic in front of you, you're living a lie. So spend time with Him when no one else is around, and let Him give you the confidence and identity you need to lead with authenticity. Give Him your heart and He'll give you His.

This book, and especially this chapter, was written from a pastor's heart. So I want to close with just a few ways our worship team at Bridges Nashville, the church I was privileged to plant and pastor for nearly 5 years, values authenticity. Feel free to take these few practical thoughts and adapt it in your context.

- We cannot place excellence above authenticity. If it looks amazing and pretty but there's nothing real and life-changing about it, then we've missed the mark. Let's do things with excellence, while staying true to who we are.
- Community offstage breeds chemistry onstage. In our community, ministry teams, small groups, and house churches, we need vulnerability and transparency. Being transparent means taking the time to be available and show real concern for others.
- What you practice in private gets magnified in public. The life of prayer and worship you live on Sundays should be from the overflow of how you live in your home.

The truth will always come out. As we saw in one of music's saddest stories with Milli Vanilli, a foundation built on lies will eventually come crashing down. Authenticity is everything. It's what God is after in our worship, in our churches, and in our everyday lives. Let's come to Him with everything—the good, the bad, the ugly. Let's allow Him to see us, heal us, build us. And as we are transformed into His image, let's lead others in doing the same.

Closing Thought

I think Kurtis hit the nail on the head in this chapter of *Worshipology*. Our authenticity is meant to overflow from our true identity as a child of God. Much like David, when we are secure of heart in our identity, then we can walk in godly confidence. Our foundation is meant to be built on knowing that we are fiercely loved by our Father and that He is always for us.

On the flip side, we tend to live inauthentically when we are disconnected from the heart of the Father. We are prone to forget that we are seen, fully known, and fully loved. The truth is, there is nothing about us that is surprising to God and nothing that is too dark or too scary to Him. We should feel so safe knowing that He unconditionally loves us. There's no striving here. We can simply rest in Him and receive our identity as sons and daughters.

For us worship leaders who serve on the platform, it can be really tempting in some of the harder seasons of life to ignore what's going on in our hearts and "fake it 'til we make it." Although there is value in staying faithful and worshiping even when we don't feel like it, we cannot ignore the pain that we are experiencing. I've found that many times, in His kindness God allows our pain to reveal a wound because He intends to bring healing.

In order to begin healing we need a fresh revelation of His heart and intentions toward us. Scripture reminds us that He is "gracious and compassionate, slow to anger and rich in love" (Ps. 145). Our words are powerful; and as simple as it sounds, a practical way we can rehearse this truth is to daily speak over ourselves "He loves me." By living in this reality, we can authentically lead ourselves and others to know Him more.

Corey Voss
Worship leader, songwriter, and artist with Integrity Music

CHAPTER 9
Excellence

I'm obsessed with sports. It goes back to my childhood. I played Little League baseball, and while playing in a game, I would be announcing the game in my head (okay, sometimes quietly under my breath). "Kurtis Parks steps up to the plate, full count, bases loaded . . ." (Hey, I had a big imagination. Still do.) Anyway, I've always loved sports. All sports. And I tried my hand at all of them. And I stunk at pretty much all of them. My brother Nate, on the other hand, is a baller and was All State in football, baseball, and track. He didn't even practice with the track team; he just showed up for the meets and won them all. He played baseball at Virginia Tech and then professionally for a little bit before joining the Army as a helicopter pilot. I've lived most of my sports dreams through Nate, and whenever we get together, we always end up talking sports.

Even though I've never been that great as a player, as a fan I'm spectacular! I truly admire athletes and their dedication and determination to be the best. According to *Business Insider*, in just about every sport, less than 2 percent of college athletes make it to the professional level. And that's if you are good enough to play in college! There's no greater display of sports excellence than the biggest global sports collective that happens every four years: the Olympics. Sorry, soccer fans, if you thought I was talking about the World Cup. In both the Winter and Summer Olympic games, the greatest athletes in the world come together to compete for just a momentary glimpse of glory, for both themselves and their country. These people train for thousands of hours, and some of their races only last 10 seconds. If that doesn't challenge you, then nothing will!

But when it comes to excellence and the Olympics, there's one name in my opinion that rises above them all. With 23 gold medals, and 28 overall medals, Michael Phelps goes down as the most decorated Olympic athlete of all time. He holds seven world records, and since he's still only in his 30s, we honestly don't know if he's finished. He stands 6'4", with a 6'7" wingspan, with size-14 flippers. However, although he definitely has a genetic edge on most people, that's not what makes him the greatest. In an interview with NBC during the 2008 Beijing Olympics, he said he ate a diet consisting of 12,000 calories a day to fuel his training efforts! But that's still not what makes him the greatest.

The reason that Michael Phelps has achieved excellence in his sport at the highest level is that he never stopped pushing himself. According to his swimming coach, Bob Bowman, Phelps followed this advice: "There can be no growth without discontent." Sociologist Daniel Chambliss, who studied the habits of Olympians, wrote a paper in 1989 titled "The Mundanity of Excellence" in which he said that repeated, consistent habits can lead to excellence. As my dad once told me, "Repetition is the key to learning." People see Phelps and chalk his success and excellence up to talent, but it's much more than that. He started swimming at the age of seven. Since his first Olympics in 2000, he's trained six hours a day, with a determination and drive to constantly be improving. He once went five straight years without missing a single day in training! In her book *Grit: The Power of Passion and Perseverance*, psychologist Angela Duckworth writes that the most successful athletes, business people, and artists aren't those who settle on raw talent, but those who are determined to work hard and put in the grind in a persistent pursuit of excellence.

As worship leaders, excellence isn't the destination. God's presence is the destination, and excellence is a road that takes us there. His presence is the end, and excellence is a means. No doubt the word "excellence" brings up a million different thoughts and interpretations, but just so we are on the same page, excellence doesn't mean perfection; it just means giving your very best. It's going all out, and all in, for what matters most in our lives. As believers and followers of Christ, we don't just strive for excellence to make our names known; we live with excellence because we live for something bigger and better than ourselves. Colossians 3:17 says, "And whatever you do, whether in word or deed, do it all in the name of the Lord Jesus, giving thanks to God the Father through him" (NIV). As you read further on in that same chapter, Paul writes, "Whatever you do, work at it with your whole being, for the Lord and not for men" (Col. 3:23, Berean). It's for *God* that we aim for excellence, and He doesn't ask for perfection. There has only been one life that ever hit the perfection target and that was Jesus'. What God asks for is our very best, from our heart, and that we don't settle for second best.

Free Solo is an incredible documentary that follows Alex Honnold as he seeks to be the first climber to ever scale El Capitan without ropes. It's pretty insane, and if you get queasy easy (say that seven times fast), it's definitely not something you should watch. The camera crew interviews Alex throughout the film and asks him why he is after such a crazy accomplishment. He says that the goal of life is to aim for perfection, and when you free-climb, you have to be perfect, or you die! I cannot imagine the pressure and anxiety that would cause, and in his case, anything less than perfect actually is death. It drove him to accomplish the highest level of excellence in his sport, but I wonder how many climbers didn't make it in the pursuit of perfection.

Excellence isn't a fear-driven thing; it's an honor-based thing. I've been in teams where the word and the concept of excellence were abused. There was an underlying fear that if we messed up in any way, sang a wrong lyric or played a wrong chord, or even wore the wrong brand of jeans (okay, I'm kidding with that one), then the consequence would be eternal banishment from the worship team and we'd never be allowed onstage again. That's not cool. Excellence isn't to be used as a weapon against people.

I've heard tales of certain celebrity worship leaders who make their bandmates pay a fee every time they mess-up onstage. Yikes. As worship leaders, we can't put that pressure on our bands, especially if they are volunteers working 40-hour-a-week jobs and then making the time to serve in our churches. If you're a worship leader who has the joy of serving full time in your church, remember to put yourself in your team members' shoes. We have single parents, full-time students, and people working in every sector of culture with all different types of pressure on them. Yes, there is a standard, and we need to make sure we set that bar and communicate the expectation well. But always remember, leading worship together is about community, not a gig. Don't put the requirement before the relationship! When you lead from community and relationship, people will put in the effort, and they will go the extra mile, because they know that they're being led in grace and truth. Truth says, "We need to be playing the right chords, singing the right lyrics, and knowing the songs." Grace says, "I understand that everyone messes up every now and then. Let's figure out what's causing that."

God is worth our best, He deserves our best, and that's why excellence matters. God gave *us* His very best when He sent His Son to be our Savior. If God held back nothing from us, then the way that we can honor Him is by giving our very best in everything that we do.

When it comes to worship, I'm reminded of the story in Genesis of two brothers. Cain and Abel had the same parents, Adam and Eve, and most likely were told the same stories growing up—stories of creation, walking in a garden alongside God, you know, the normal stuff. When it came time for them to atone for their sins, they both knew the requirement: to offer God the first and best. While Abel followed that command and was looked upon with favor, Cain decided to play by his own rules. And if you read the story, you know what happened. Cain became a vagabond, running for his life as a marked man.

This story from Genesis might not have obvious worship implications, but I find it a powerful call to worship leaders. Don't bring God a "Cain offering." When we bring our very best to what we do, it's truly a sacrifice. A sacrifice costs you something. It's painful sometimes, and in our modern day of convenience, we don't like something that's not easy. Thankfully we live in the New Covenant made through Christ, so animal sacrifice is no longer a requirement. But there is still a sacrifice that is asked of us. Romans 12:1 says, "Therefore, I urge you, brothers and sisters, in view of God's mercy, to offer your bodies as a living sacrifice, holy and pleasing to God—this is your true and proper worship."

In Scripture, sacrifice is always used in the context of worship. Our very lives are to be a sacrifice to God—living in constant surrender to Christ's lordship and being a vessel to be used by the Holy Spirit. This is our sacrifice. The writer of Hebrews puts it this way: "Through Jesus, therefore, let us continually offer to God a sacrifice of praise—the fruit of lips that openly profess his name" (Heb. 13:15). The Greek word for "sacrifice" (*thysian*) in this verse means "offering," so this is like our

New Covenant version of the Old Testament animal sacrifices. And it happens with praise. It's just a lot less bloody.

How can we bring anything less than our very best and expect God to bless that? Honoring the Lord is the main reason we go for excellence. The human reason for why you should pursue excellence? It's just a lot more fun that way! Have you ever finished a set of songs with a band that gave their best, played incredibly, and smashed every chord, where the drums crushed the beat, and all the harmonies were slamming? It's a blast! It's like a football team that practiced all week and then went out on the field and came away with a victory. It's just plain fun. And something that becomes fun is something you'll want more of. When you taste excellence, you start to go after it more, because you know how much fun and sweet it can be. If we become excellent at leading our church in worshiping the King, then we'll want to do that all the time. It's about the worship of the King, not the excellence of His people. But they go together like peanut butter and jelly.

There is also an attractive quality to excellence that should draw people in. It should get people excited to be a part of something *good!* As a singer or musician, doesn't it just feel great to be on a team that cares about what they're doing? Anything else is just a waste of time. Your congregation will also notice a difference in a band that has put in the time to bring their best and a band that was poorly put together.

Excellence is something that our culture understands: only the best make it to the top. People value excellence in everything—the movies we watch, the food we eat, the products we buy. We have the Grammys to award the best singers, producers, and songwriters. We have the Oscars to award the greatest movies. There are reality competitions on TV in every category that give the prize to excellence. My wife and I are huge *Survivor* fans, and the person who wins the million-dollar prize has to be excellent in the way they play the game, socially, physically, and mentally—anything less and "the tribe has spoken!"

I love the "just okay" commercials from AT&T. My favorite is where someone goes in for surgery and the nurse claims that the doctor performing the surgery is "just okay." A look of terror shoots into the eyes of the patient and his family. You wouldn't want to be on the scalpel side of an "okay" doctor. You wouldn't move into a house that was built by an "okay" construction team.

Our culture knows excellence, and you can't reach a culture if you don't speak their language. It should give you pause when you think about the first-time guest, the one who has never been to church before, walking through our doors. The way they're greeted in the beginning is major. Do they encounter smiling faces welcoming them, or do they feel like an uninvited guest who isn't allowed to be a part of the cool kids club?

I've read several studies that show that a person will decide whether or not they will come back to your church in the first seven minutes. When this guest enters the sanctuary and the service kicks off, what is usually the first part of any church service? Worship music! Before the pastor comes up to preach, music will greet their ears. You could be someone's first impression of Jesus. In a moment of worship, a hard heart can melt like wax, a person's false perception of the Church can crumble, and the Spirit of God can begin to ride on the sound of worship and cut to the soul. And *this* is one reason why excellence matters.

You and I both know that we live in a world that is filled with distractions. Anything can take people out of a moment because of our easily diverted minds. A mistake onstage can lead to a distraction offstage. This charge to excellence applies to sound and production teams as well. They have the responsibility of making sure there's no feedback and that the mix is the best it can be. You could have the most talented and anointed band onstage, but if the mix is horrible, the end result will fall short.

We're called to excellence in everything we do because we're made in the image of a God who pours out excellence. *Yahweh* (the Hebrew name for God) translates as "I AM." There's nothing greater, no one higher; at the end of the day, "I AM" is everything. In creation, God showed His mastery in design by the way He crafted the world together. Everything was set in perfect order, with nothing out of balance. Jesus was the spoken Word, and through Him all things were created (see John 1:3); the Holy Spirit was hovering over the chaos, holding all things together (see Gen. 1:2). Even the way the Trinity exists in perfect harmony is a sign of the excellence of heaven. Whew, I get goosebumps!

If God didn't care about excellence, then we wouldn't have Exodus! In this book, we see God giving Moses the instructions for the Tabernacle in intricate detail. God gives the blueprint for an excellent life through the Ten Commandments. Everything God creates and sets in order is done without flaw—including creating you and me. Psalm 139 says that we are "fearfully and wonderfully made." God doesn't make mistakes. When we bring our best to Him, it's a way of showing our love and honor to the God who deserves it all! I often tell our team that excellence sets the table for worship. Are we setting the table with fine china or plasticware?

When you look throughout Scripture, you find excellence all over the place. David was known for his skills on a harp. That's how he got from the pasture to the palace.

> So Saul said to his attendants, "Find someone who plays well and bring him to me." One of the servants answered, "I have seen a son of Jesse of Bethlehem who knows how to play the lyre. He is a brave man and a warrior. He speaks well and is a fine-looking man. And the Lord is with him." Then Saul sent messengers to Jesse and said, "Send me your son David, who is with the sheep." So Jesse took a donkey loaded with bread, a skin of wine and a young goat and sent them with his son David to Saul. David came to Saul and entered his service. Saul liked him very much, and David became one of his armor-bearers. Then Saul sent word to Jesse, saying, "Allow David to remain in my service, for I am pleased with him." Whenever the spirit from God came on Saul, David would take up his lyre and play. Then relief would come to Saul; he would feel better, and the evil spirit would leave him. (1 Sam. 16:17-23)

David got in front of royalty by his reputation for excellence. It was something that stuck with him his whole life. In fact, he would only bring the best of the best in to play music when he was the king. First Chronicles 25 is a list of the "who's who" of the rock bands of ancient Israel:

> All these men were under the supervision of their father for the music of the temple of the Lord, with cymbals, lyres, and harps, for the ministry at the house of God. Asaph, Jeduthun and Heman were under the supervision of the king. Along with their relatives—all of them trained and skilled in music for the Lord—they numbered 288. (1 Chron. 25:6-7)

"Trained and skilled"—that's how you got to play at the temple. David wrote the words "play skillfully" in Psalm 33:3. The Hebrew word for "skillfully" means to be "pleasing"; another translation has "to make it beautiful." David was known by all of Israel as someone who not only cared about excellence but also lived it out in everything he did. Psalm 78, written by someone other than David, can attest to this: "And David shepherded them with integrity of heart; with skillful hands he led them" (v. 72). That's a good leadership model right there: integrity and excellence. He had character and talent. It takes both to lead well.

So, when it comes to musical worship, why do we settle for okay if we know we can bring a higher level? I cringe anytime I hear the following phrases from worship leaders: "I didn't have time to look over the songs," "What key are we doing this in?" or "How does this guitar part go?" We have to set a higher bar if we want to reach a higher level of excellence in our churches and on our teams. Don't set that bar in fear but in admiration. Let excellence be something that we run toward, not a consequence that we run from.

First and foremost, it has to be the standard that *you* as a leader set. You can't ask your team to be somewhere that you're not willing to go. If you're not at a place where you can lead with skill, then you have two options: get there, or get someone else who *is* there. I believe you can't have excellence without evaluation. Often you need to start that evaluation process with yourself. Maybe you don't have the best voice; so take voice lessons. Maybe you're not playing the right strum patterns or chord phrasings; so practice guitar.

As a leader you cannot expect to play and lead with skill if you only pick up your instrument on Sundays. I've made that mistake, and it's not pretty. There have been weeks when the set list was songs that I've played before a hundred times, so I didn't think I needed to review them before the weekend. Well, I looked pretty silly leading a band in pre-service rehearsal through songs that I was singing wrong lyrics to and messing up the arrangement. Listen, I mess up the lyrics to songs that I've written! So I definitely know I need to honor the process by practicing before I get onstage. And so do you. First, be honest with where you are personally on the skill scale. Here are a few things you can do right now to help you raise your standard of excellence as a leader:

Keep It Simple

I've lived my life by the motto "excellence meets simplicity." Don't set 20 different goals for yourself, because you'll most likely fail at 20 different things. You can't be great at everything, but you can be great at a few things. So keep it simple, keep it attainable, and make the necessary steps toward accomplishing the goal. Small steps, one at a time, toward improving anything is the best method to being sure you accomplish it! If you want to be better at leading while playing an instrument, start practicing and singing at the same time while at home. If you're always rushing or slowing down the tempo, start practicing with a metronome or click track. I often tell my team, "Know what you *can* do onstage and crush it. Know what you *can't* do and work on it at home." Some of the greatest songwriters out there never use more than four chords in a song. We all can name at least 30 worship songs that have stood the test of time using this philosophy. Less really is more. So keep it simple.

Let the Record Show

I highly recommend recording yourself to know where you need to grow. Sometimes when I'm trying to nail a guitar part, I'll play along to the song and record it and go back to listen. Recordings don't lie. Record a rehearsal and listen to it with your team. You may even find it fun to do this *as* a team, listening and asking people where they can find spots to improve. Music is a craft, and recording puts it under a microscope so you can fine-tune it.

It's the same with video. A while back I had a protégé who was studying underneath me to learn and grow in their worship skill and leadership. Each weekend I would place them at a different campus of our church to lead. I'd always ask on Mondays, "How was it?" To which they replied, "It was amazing!" But I was hearing different responses from a few of the team members and pastors. So I said to my protégé, "Let's get the next service on video. I'd love to see how you're leading." After recording that Sunday, we got together to watch the service. You can probably guess what he said: "That was awful." I didn't even have to say anything, because video doesn't lie!

I never record any of our team or leaders as a fear tactic; it's only as a mechanism to improve. Think about how an NFL team goes into the locker room on Monday to watch game footage from their weekend match. They're studying to see what went right, what went wrong, and how they can do better next time. The same is true in recording a worship team. Musically, and even pastorally, as leaders we can always move forward. I've had times when I listened to a worship set and heard a teaching moment in between songs when it seemed like I was just rambling incoherent thoughts. I knew what I was *trying* to say, but it didn't come out that way. So I started writing down my teaching moments and talking through them ahead of time. You can't have excellence without evaluation!

Have a Mentor

We all need someone who pushes us in our craft. Just like a newbie in the gym wants a trainer to get them doing the right thing, so too we all need a person "spotting" us in the musical gym. People often settle for mediocrity when there's no one pushing them to greatness! Even after Aaron Rodgers won a Super Bowl with the Green Bay Packers, when he was asked in an interview what he was looking for, he answered, "I desperately want to be coached!" We can always be better and further along than where we are. So find someone who can help get you to where you want to be. This might even be a musician or singer on your team.

When I was touring with my band The Season, we had a guitarist, Josh, who was one of the best musicians I've ever been around. At the time I was really stepping into playing electric guitar and trying to understand tone. I got around Josh as much as I could and put myself in a posture of learning. Music is a muscle, and I wanted to get stronger!

There's also the spiritual side of having a coach. Leaders are called to inspire and challenge those who they are leading. If you are a leader reading this book, my question to you is, who is challenging and inspiring you? We all need people who call out our potential, musically and spiritually. Is there someone who is discipling you? A pastor, or someone who is further down the road with Jesus? Who is the iron to *your* iron (see Prov. 27:17)?

Learning Is Growing

The moment you think you've got it all figured out is the moment God will prove you wrong! This is why we always need to be students of our craft. In the worship world, who is a teacher you can learn from? There could be another worship leader in your community or city who has led worship for decades. I would encourage you to get coffee or lunch with that person.

Books are a gift! There are many books out there that were written to grow you, so go and discover some incredible authors and see where people have been challenged. And don't just read books on music and worship. Read books that deepen your love for Christ and your desire for His presence. I have grown tremendously as a worship leader from reading authors that I'll probably never get the chance to meet, at least on this side of eternity. Writings by A. W. Tozer and C. S. Lewis have shaped my theology. I've also read books by worship artists like Matt Redman, David Crowder, and Bob Kauflin that have been monumental in my walk with Jesus.

Conferences are another great way to sharpen your skills. There are dozens of worship conferences every year all across the globe. You'll hear new methods, viewpoints, discoveries, and best of all, you'll meet new friends! I've gone to conferences and come away with solid relationships that have helped me grow as a follower of Christ. You bump into different anointings when you go to worship conferences. It's a picture of the unity in diversity throughout the global church! You'll chat with leaders who have a different style than yours, and oftentimes you'll get a bigger glimpse of what God is doing in the Church at large, the body of Christ. It's inspiring! It's often easy to put our blinders on and only think about our team and our church 100 percent of the time. Conferences give you a bigger perspective. One caution about conferences though: they can often leave you feeling overwhelmed. I've walked away and felt discouraged that my team could never be on that level. I've also felt like I heard so much information that I didn't know where to begin. This is why it's always important to take it in, process it, and find one or two key takeaways that you can begin to implement in your team.

Consistency Is Key

Aristotle said, "We are what we repeatedly do. Excellence, then, is not an act, but a habit." You can't expect to practice for an hour on piano and then automatically start playing Beethoven. You also can't expect to write one song and have a chart topping hit on your hands. You have to keep at it. I've written more than 1,200 songs in my life. That sounds impressive, but when you understand that 90 percent of those songs will never make it out of my bedroom, you know what I'm all about. The more I write, the better I get. And with that commitment to consistency is the understanding that it takes time. They didn't build Rome in a day, and you can't build excellence in a day. Excellence isn't a microwave; it's a crockpot. It takes time and commitment. As I've said before, my dad often tells me, "Repetition is the key to learning." Commit to the process and don't give up!

When you're ready to lead a team into excellence, share the steps that got you to where you are. I want to share five quick thoughts to close out this chapter on excellence, and I think they can be tweaked and used in whatever setting you're in and in any team dynamic. Feel free to use what you can, and chuck the rest out the door. You won't hurt my feelings. Just don't tell me.

1. Start With What You Have

I love the fact that Jesus didn't wait until His disciples were fully sanctified and prepared before doing ministry with them. He found guys who were willing and able, and then they went to work! Similarly, we have to start with where we are and who we have on our teams. So, if it's just one person on acoustic, or maybe you hit the jackpot and have a drummer, go with that Black Keys style for a bit. Don't feel like you need to have *more* people on your team; you just need the *right* people on your team. Oftentimes the right people are those who have humble hearts, willing attitudes, and a work ethic to match.

I've been to a worship service that had one dude on piano and it was more powerful than a bunch of times I've seen full bands. You can have excellence at any phase as you build, but know that it's harder to back-track to excellence. Here's what I mean. If you have a bunch of "just okay" musicians on drums, bass, keys, then you're going to have a less than okay sound, because you'll only be as strong as your weakest link. They'll be working harder with less output. But if you start smaller, with, say, one amazing acoustic guitarist and a vocalist, then they can create a sound that has a solid foundation to build off of. Think about Ed Sheeran – just one guy with a guitar and a loop pedal, and it's amazing. Then when you have that drummer or piano player who comes in, you have something strong to build on. If you really want to have that full-band sound, you can utilize resources like Ableton or MainStage to fill out the sound with backing tracks. Just remember that you'll need the right setup, and your players will need to be solid with click and guide tracks.

2. Define Excellence in Your Context

People's ideas of great are all over the spectrum, so you need to map out what excellence looks like in your specific context. If you're in a small town without a massive pool of Berkeley-trained musicians, then you will have a different definition. That's okay. Remember, excellence isn't perfection; it's simply your very best. Playing to click, playing the parts for electric guitar, vocalists singing with the right tone, pitch and harmony blend—these are all steps toward excellence.

Define and communicate your expectations for your team. Auditions are very helpful in this matter. They help you set the standard. Auditions are a natural filter to put more emphasis on excellence, and in the long run it'll take out some headaches. You might not get as many people on the team, but you'll get the right ones who will bring their A game to the team. Just by saying "you have to audition," a lot of people won't make that step because they don't even have the commitment to learn a couple songs for the audition. I've had people tell me they've toured with major label artists and have been playing their instrument for 20 years, but when they came for the audition, they couldn't play a simple chord chart, because they didn't put any time in with the song. You can't wing it on a team, and an audition will show you what someone's dedication is!

3. Have a Rehearsal

I can't stress how huge of a step this is. It's hard to expect excellence from your team when you don't create the space for it. Rehearsals are the perfect space to nail down the arrangements, walk through the transitions (often an overlooked part of the worship set), and let your band get comfortable with each other, their instruments, and their monitor mix. Even if you use tracks with your team, having a rehearsal gives your people an added layer of confidence going into the weekend, knowing that they've been there, done that.

Having a midweek practice run gives you the chance to make any changes to arrangements that aren't flowing or keys that aren't working right for the singers. If you wait until the day of to do all that, chances are you'll not catch everything pre-service, creating a recipe for a trainwreck! We've all had those mornings when it took an extra 30 minutes to set up or the sound check went late, and the last thing you have time for is rehearsal. Take the pressure off having to squeeze all that into a short amount of time, and give the extra space needed to hit excellence. If you have a midweek rehearsal, you also give your team time to work through and live with the songs. Maybe they had a certain part in mind but it didn't work in practice. Now they have a few days to think through their parts and come into the weekend solid.

Rehearsals are also a great place to practice flow or spontaneous worship. That might sound weird to see "practice" and "spontaneous" in the same sentence. I was in a small room of worship leaders several years back listening to some of Hillsong's worship team. Jad Gilles explained that many of the moments they have in their concerts that may feel like spontaneous expressions were actually built on hours of rehearsal. What he was saying is that the team knows the songs and the set so well that when the Holy Spirit wants to breathe on a particular moment, they are ready for it. In rehearsal, you get the chance to go there with no one watching. Rehearsals let you try different things, with the freedom to fail. If a bridge idea or a drum break works in rehearsal, give it a shot on Sunday. If not, no big deal.

On the discipleship side, rehearsals give you another time and space to build relationship and leverage community. During worship team rehearsals with Bridges Nashville, we close out our time with sharing prayer requests, and it's always a beautiful time of lifting one another's arms and bearing each other's burdens (see Gal. 6:2). We often open up our time of practice with a quick devotional or a psalm. We may even share the thought process behind picking the certain songs for that week's set. Often, if I'm a part of the worship team, I tell them from a pastoral side why we chose the songs we did. It gives a bigger perspective and vision to the team that we're not just playing songs; we're leading worship!

If you're reading this and not currently at a place where your team is rehearsing weekly, I highly encourage you to make that a priority. For more than the reasons listed above, these will take you to another level. If you have too much on your plate, what can you take off your plate to make rehearsal a priority? Is there a layer to your responsibility that you can delegate so that you can make this important step? Rehearsals can only better the level of your team!

4. Grow Together

You can't expect your team to grow if you never give them the resources or opportunities to do so. One way to give your team the opportunity to improve is through breakout sessions and instrumental or vocal clinics. This is when you bring someone who is an expert in their craft to pour out into your team. We've done this with guitarists, where we brought in someone who has played on well-known albums to share their knowledge about tone and technique. We've had vocal coaches come in and give our singers practice methods and vocal tips. We've had drummers, songwriters, bassists, and keyboard players all conduct workshops. Doing something like this brings your team together, and it gets them talking together about their craft. Oftentimes after a clinic, I'll see musicians going out to lunch and building community. Whenever you get your team together on the grounds of excellence, the house of community is built! Having someone outside your church come in to lead a clinic is also wise, because their words can carry weight on topics that you may have had a hard time addressing.

The funny thing is, many times, whoever is teaching the clinic will often say things that I've said a hundred times, but because it's coming from a fresh voice and through a new lens, my team members will finally connect the dots! If you are the only voice your team is hearing from and learning from, eventually you run the risk of becoming white noise! But just like a classroom makes you smarter, a workshop can raise the bar of excellence. Aim to host one or two of these over the next year, and see how your team responds! If you don't have the budget to bring in a well-trained musician or vocal coach, start with what you have! Maybe there is an amazing drummer in your town, or even in a local cover band, who could come and sit with your drummers for a morning. Buy them a Starbucks gift card and give them the opportunity to share some wisdom on their playing. You're not asking them to do a class on theology! Or you may have six or seven bass players on your team. Find the player who has the most knowledge and a teaching skill set, and give them the ownership of leading a clinic. It gives them a voice and honors their value.

5. Less Is More

Another practical idea is to implement a song bank. This is something we've done at Bridges Nashville, and we did it at National Community Church in my time there as worship director. It wasn't my original idea, and at first I didn't like it because it felt a bit restrictive and usually meant fewer songs to choose from. But I learned that those songs were always done at the highest level.

Here's how it works: for a season (two to three months), pick out songs that you want to lead in your church. We would usually pick 25-30 songs that hit a wide variety of topics, tempos, and styles. You can pick songs that go with the sermon series, songs that you want your church to sing based on the theology behind it, and songs that fit the particular season God has your church in. Then be wise in picking songs for tempo and feel. You don't want 25 slow songs. That's going to be a boring three months. I usually will find a good mix of fast, mid-tempo, and slow songs. Throw some hymns in there, and if you write songs for your church, toss in some originals.

What this does is make it easier for your team to know a group of songs. Put together a Spotify or YouTube playlist, and encourage your team to get the songs in their hearts. You'll find that a lot of your team, especially the high-level players, will memorize the songs. It's a huge bonus when by the second or third time in that season your band has the songs down by heart. It might feel like you're restricting yourself, but you're actually freeing up your team to be their best. It's *freedom within framework.* Also the reality of having 25 songs for three months is that even if you're at a church that sings four songs every Sunday, you'd have to go six weeks of playing new songs before you even run into the possibility of a repeat! Choosing the song bank can be a fun process for your leaders, vocalists, and pastors. So make sure that it's not just your ego choosing songs that you prefer. Have a mix of people in the room when implementing a song bank.

One final way to step into excellence wherever you are is to just *play fewer songs* until your team is ready to handle more. If you're not at the place where you can have a midweek rehearsal, maybe instead of five songs every Sunday with a ton of chord changes, you can condense it into something your team can handle. Maybe two or three songs with simple structures that you can run through on a Sunday pre-service. As a congregation member, I'd rather be led in two songs that are done beautifully than five songs that sound like a trainwreck. The cool thing is, you'll start to get better as a team when you go for less.

Remember, every pathway to excellence is lined by a bunch of small steps. As my father-in-law, Pete, tells me, "How do you eat an elephant? One bite at a time." Then you can build off that simple foundation. Excellence meets simplicity. I don't think I've ever heard someone complain about a church service being too short. I *have* heard the opposite! Do what you can handle well, even if it's just a few songs, then graduate to more advanced songs and deeper bands when you have the time, energy, and space to add a rehearsal. The other bonus of all these steps to excellence is having people in your congregation step out of the shadows because *now* they see a team worth joining. People want to be a part of something that is *good*. If you have a poor worship experience over and over, it won't attract musicians who want to be a part of something special. A worship service done from our very best won't necessarily attract new people to your church, but I can guarantee that a poor sound will always repel people! Bring your best; it's all God asks for!

When you aim for excellence with the right motive, you'll get the right results. God's character, design, and love for us all breathe excellence. He does everything with incredible thought and precision. We honor God with the way we worship. I love that Augustine said, "Pray as though everything depended on God. Work as though everything depended on you."

When you bring your best, you are giving God a sacrifice of praise, an offering He looks on with favor. I close with the lyrics from one of my favorite Christmas songs, "Little Drummer Boy" (minus all the *pa rum pums*):

> I played my drum for him
> I played my best for him
> Then he smiled at me
> Me and my drum

Closing Thought

The Old Testament law designs a relentlessly detailed order to Jewish worship. The Tabernacle and the temple were places of order where experienced and educated priests would meticulously execute their duties with precision. I often think of excellence as an extension of that Old Testament tradition. As we commit attention to the details of a worship experience, we echo the practices of our priestly ancestors. More than the apparent practical application, excellence roots us in the biblical tradition as well.

As a worship pastor, my commitment to excellence helps my ministry because it offers more ways to interact with the students I work with. Staying after hours to work on a part, or practicing warm-ups to a metronome—these are ways I can connect with the people serving alongside me in ministry. Sometimes I think of the days I spent after school with the basketball team. The skill work behind the scenes helped our performance in games, but the unexpected consequence of practice is the growth we experience in our relationships. Excellence is part of our tradition as pastors, and it's also a way to practically build the communities we're called to.

Daniel Rivera
Worship pastor and songwriter, SEU Worship

CHAPTER 10
Sing a New Song

Sing to the Lord a new song; sing o the Lord all the earth.
Psalm 96:1

Why Should We Write?

Six times throughout the book of Psalms, we read the phrase "sing a new song." It wasn't just a lyric; it was a lesson. David, Asaph, Ethan, the sons of Korah, and other songwriters were writing to capture the story of God and to be able to pass it along to the next generation in a way that they wouldn't easily forget—song. There are epic moments throughout Scripture when God's commandments are taught and caught through melodies. I have a simple equation I've shared throughout this book when it comes to this: message + music = memory.

In Deuteronomy 32, Moses, as he's coming to the end of his life, teaches the nation of Israel a tune to help them remember all the goodness and ways of the Lord. It's a 43-verse song that ends with a lesson on how to pass it on:

> Moses came with Joshua son of Nun and spoke all the words of this song in the hearing of the people. When Moses finished reciting all these words to all Israel, he said to them, "Take to heart all the words I have solemnly declared to you this day, so that you may command your children to obey carefully all the words of this law. They are not just idle words for you—they are

your life. By them you will live long in the land you are crossing
the Jordan to possess." (Deut. 32:44-47)

Not bad for a guy of 120 years. Songwriting leaves a legacy that
outlives your days on Earth. That song would be sung as the people of
God took the land of promise. I can imagine some *kumbaya* moments
around the ancient campfire, singing the song of Moses.

Songwriting was also a trade passed down from one generation
to another. Much like carpenters and farmers taught their sons and
daughters the family business, so too King David had songwriting in
his family tree. David is without a doubt the best-known songwriter in
Scripture, but I'm not sure he was the most prolific. Solomon, his son,
wrote more than 1,000 songs, not to mention 3,000 proverbs, according to 1 Kings 4:32. But who's counting?

Fast-forward to the AD era and you see Paul telling the Church to
teach through "psalms, hymns, and songs of the Spirit." Songwriting
gives us the opportunity to teach theology with music as the method.
So the question then becomes, what do you need to teach? This will
drive the reason you need to write. Obviously I know that not everyone
who reads this is called to be a songwriter, but if you do feel that stirring
to begin to write songs, first and foremost ask God to illuminate what
you need to write. Long before I wrote songs, I was writing poetry; so
maybe that's where you start. In this chapter I'll give some practical
ways to step into songwriting; but before we go there, I'd like to offer a
few additional reasons to write songs for your church.

It's in Our Nature to Create

All of us were made to be creative. In his book *Let Me Out*, Peter
Himmelman writes about a tribe in East Africa that incorporates music
and tribal singing into most everything they do. One of Himmelman's
friends was visiting the tribe for research when they asked him to join
in the song. He bashfully replied, "I don't sing." It was incomprehensi-
ble to the tribe, not even in their vocab, that someone couldn't sing. It
wasn't an option. Singing was life.

For many of us, the words "I can't" are the enemy of creativity.
Somewhere down the line we stop dreaming, we stop imagining, we
stop creating. The average toddler asks 200 questions a day. Once you
reach adulthood, that number drops to around six! Pablo Picasso said,

"When I was a child, I painted as a master; now as a man, I strive to paint like a child." We are all born with creativity. It always gets a little under my skin when people single out "creatives" in a room. A musician who writes a theme, an author who writes a blog, a teacher who comes up with curriculum, an artist who paints, a mechanic who fixes, a gardener who plants, a fashion designer who sews, an accountant who reports—creativity lies within all of us. "Whatever you do, do unto the glory of God. Whatever you do, work at it with all your heart, as working for the Lord, not for human masters" (Col. 3:23).

We are created in the image of a creative God, who spoke the light into being and the earth into existence with the sound of His voice. One group of Hebrew scholars believes that those cosmic words weren't just spoken—they were sung. It's believed that in the Garden of Eden, all of creation sang and all things were in harmony, not just in the hippie way, but in a sonic way. God is the original songwriter, and you are one of His masterpieces. So creativity is in your family gene pool. "Creative" isn't just reserved for the entertainment industry. I try to encourage all worship leaders to give songwriting a shot. Pick up a guitar or sit at the piano and ask God for a download from heaven.

Heart Song

Sometimes we can only sing what our hearts want to say. Music is where raw emotion meets pure expression. When you write a song, you can sometimes get out on paper what you want to say to God, or to another person, that mere conversation fails to convey. When you put melody to lyric, it takes off in a way that puts a soundtrack to your worship. When leading worship, I've often seen that a song can give word and expression to people when they don't really know what to say to God. Songs can often be the Hallmark card for people to pick out and offer to God in worship. Whether it's a song of repentance, joy, or praise, a song gives wings to our words and expression from the heart.

Recital for Papa

God wants to hear your song. Just as unique as every person's story is, so too is the song that we have to sing—or for some of us, the song we have *yet* to sing. But God loves to hear His kids sing, especially an original song. "Because he bends down to listen, I will pray as long as I have breath!" (Ps. 116:2). God leans down to hear us when we pray and when we put those prayers to melody.

When my kids were really little, they would come to me with dances that they had made up. There was the "duck dance," "the monkey dance," and even the "poopoo dance." You can guess which one was my favorite. It was totally spontaneous, made up on the spot, and they just wanted me to watch. Then they would wait for my approval and applause. I think that so often we are afraid to put originality out there because of rejection. What if people don't like this song? What if it's not good? I can promise that there will always be criticism when you release creativity. Don't worry about the haters; do it for your Maker! I can also promise that when you sing from a heart of worship to your Father in heaven, rejection is the last thing on His mind.

Write for Your Church

What is the story God is writing in your church? One of the best ways to steward His story is by writing a song. In the churches I've served at on staff, I charge our worship team to take the series that our pastors were teaching and write "songs for series." Oftentimes our pastors would lend us sermon notes that turned into lyric fuel. Writing a song out of a teaching series let that message outlive the series. Whenever we sang that original song, it would bring back the scriptures, testimonies, and quotable quips from that sermon series.

Early on in my time as the lead pastor of Bridges Nashville, I wrote a song with one of our worship leaders, Delaney Ramsdell, called "Start Again" that was based on a series we did called "Comeback Story." The takeaway from those messages was that it's never too late to be who God created you to be. The song "Start Again" was all about finding a fresh beginning and living as a new creation, from 2 Corinthians 5:17. It was the first single we released, and we sing it regularly now. Other churches have started to sing it as well, taking the story beyond our walls. It's beautiful to think that a song that started as an idea in a writing room is now giving fresh expression to people in worship!

You can also write a song out of someone's personal story, with their permission of course. I was once asked to write a song for someone who had recently lost her father to a battle with cancer. She told me his personality, his quirks, and the things she missed the most about him. It was one of the most emotional songs I've ever written, but when I sent it to her, I'll never forget the response. Tears filled her eyes as she remembered her dad in a unique way. You can write a song out of your own testimony as well, which leads me to my next point.

Write for Yourself

Much like journaling, songwriting is a way to mark a season of your life. What is God speaking to your heart? Oftentimes His work in your life may help someone else discover His work in theirs. Writing helps what's on the inside come out and puts your feelings on paper. I'd encourage you to be totally fine if you and God are the only ones who hear that song. Songwriting can be therapeutic, and it can be a way that God uses to bring closure to difficult things you may be walking through. I highly doubt David knew at the time he wrote Psalm 23 that it would go on to be one of the most famous songs in the world. He wrote that out of his personal journey with God. It's been quoted in church services, funerals, and in more songs than I can count! David didn't write for royalties; he wrote for emotional release.

Sadly, many worship leaders can get eyes bigger than their church and start to write songs with the motivation of getting the next hit. I've been there, done that, and have the T-shirt to prove it. Okay, I don't really have the T-shirt, but there was a time when I got obsessed with writing the next number-one worship song, and it drove me to self-centered songwriting. It was less about glorifying God and more about promoting me. That's a bad place to be, and you'll have nothing but rotten fruit come out of it. Thank God for His kindness that leads us to repentance.

Now that we've highlighted some good reasons to write songs, I want to get super practical on how to jump into the world of songwriting.

Where Do You Start?

When you first have the desire to start anything new in your life, it's easy to get lost in the end results and overlook the process that it takes to get there. For every visible outcome, there are multiple unseen inputs to get there. We tune in to the Olympics and see a world-class athlete taking home the gold medal, not thinking of the endless hours, days, and years he or she trained to get to the big stage. We see someone in politics delivering a speech that inspires (or enrages) millions without realizing teams were put together just to edit the speech. We hear a chart-topping song on the radio without seeing the writing, producing, recording, and marketing portion of the music industry. We see the end, but we don't always see the road traveled to get there!

The same thing happens in songwriting. It's easy to dream about writing music, but the process of giving a song skin and bones is a different ball game. Every song starts as a dream, a thought, an idea. But then you have to put sweat and hard work to that dream to make it a reality. Robert Herjavec, of *Shark Tank* fame, once said, "A goal without a deadline is just a dream." Songs won't write themselves.

When it comes down to the basics, a song is *lyric plus melody*. The melody has to be singable and catchy, and the lyric has to really mean something. Don't write without a purpose! If you have a cool phrase that keeps resonating in your mind, almost like something you could hashtag on Twitter, then you might have a lyric starting point. If you have a melody that you can't get out of your head, that seems to almost annoy you because it's so catchy, you probably have a musical starting point! Quick side note: if you can't find the harmony to your melody, chances are it's not a good one!

If you don't have a melody or lyric, then start with a theme. What is God doing in your life that you have to sing about? Six different times throughout the book of Psalms, we read, "Sing a new song to the Lord." God is always doing something new, and in most instances what He is currently doing in your life will be the most real experience you can write from. Maybe you're going through a tough season and need to write about suffering. Maybe you're going through uncertainty and need to write about wrestling with faith and doubt. On the flip side, you could be experiencing a ton of victory and joy, so write out of that place.

Once you have the idea, lyric, or melody, start to work it out. Think about your audience, who you are singing to. Is it for God, for your church, for your spouse? Or maybe it's just a song that you need to write as a prayer to God. There's absolutely nothing wrong with a song that only hits your ears and God's. Much like a drawing that my kids give me, sometimes the sweetest gift to the Father is something His kids craft just for Him. As I've said before, I've written more than 1,200 songs and the majority of my songs haven't made it out of my living room. Out of those 1,200 songs, only a small percentage have been sung in churches or made it onto albums, with even less getting to radio.

For the sake of speaking to worship leaders, when it comes to writing worship, a song can take a horizontal direction (sung to the people of God) or a vertical direction (sung to the heart of God). I personally think we'll never have enough songs *to* God, telling Him how amazing He is and thanking Him for all He's done through Christ. We need more songs about the Holy Spirit and more songs telling of the wonder and awe of the cross and the resurrection life. We'll never have enough songs about the love of God or the saving grace of Jesus. On the other side of that coin, writing a song for the church is a powerful way of instilling identity and encouraging the body of Christ.

Think about who you are writing the song to, and be sure to stay in that frame of reference. There's nothing more confusing than a song that jumps around in both tense and reference.

Editing Is Song Stewardship

As you work out the song, remember: we tend to finish things too quickly. We sometimes rush art, and we end up with something subpar, a product of our gifting that doesn't do justice to the gift. Sometimes we would rather be done than do something well. Great work takes time. Don't be afraid to edit, rework, and rewrite. Leonard Cohen's song "Hallelujah" has been named one of the 500 greatest songs of all time by *Rolling Stone* magazine. *Q* magazine named it among the top-ten all-time greatest tracks. It has nearly 300 different versions, with covers done by Bob Dylan, Willie Nelson, Bono, and of course Jeff Buckley. *Blender* magazine even named it the greatest song of all time. But it's little known that the four-verse song that has become a part of pop royalty started out with 80 drafted verses. Editing is key to creativity.

The song needs to make sense and it needs to tell a story. A song is often a conversation or a story put to rhyme and melody. When writing worship, don't go Shakespearean. Sing it like you would say it. If you have to sing your song like Yoda would talk just to make it rhyme, you probably need to keep working on the lyrics. Particular to writing worship songs is the ability to pray the lyrics. Worship is prayer put to melody, so can you pray your song? Use imagery, use Scripture, and use story. One of the reasons country music is a best-selling genre is its storytelling aspect of it. The writers paint pictures and transport you to a time or a place. They put the listener into the story. At Bridges Nashville, we have the privilege of meeting at the Listening Room Café, one of Music City's most popular songwriter spots. I love popping in for a show and hearing the stories through song. In worship, we can't settle for halfway, half-hearted songs.

Imagery is used throughout the Psalms.

- Psalm 42:1—"As the deer longs for streams of water, so I long for you, O God."
- Psalm 148:3—"Praise him, sun and moon! Praise him, all you twinkling stars!"

Every verse in Psalm 23 paints a picture. And as the old adage goes, "a picture paints a thousand words."

So Fresh and So Clean

Step up to the challenge of writing something different and making the familiar new. One of the most common themes in songwriting across every genre is love. And yet songs are written nearly every day containing new ways to say "I love you." When writing worship songs, we get to illuminate the Word of God and highlight the character of God. A song like "Good Good Father" is so simple, and yet it connects with so many people because it shows that even if our earthly parents aren't the greatest, we all have a perfect heavenly Father. A song like "Reckless Love" by Cory Asbury connects with so many people because it paints a raw image of God's love that will chase us down, destroying any lie or wall that stands in His way. As a songwriter, I always want to leave the audience with something they didn't know before, or maybe it's something they knew but are now thinking about in a fresh way.

Give It Structure

I heard a brilliant songwriter once say, "Write a chorus and make that your verse. Write another chorus and make it your bridge. Write another chorus and make that your chorus." You see, the chorus has to be the anchor of the song, and it needs to be so strong that it ties it all together. Make every part great, and make the chorus that anchor of greatness!

A song needs structure. Don't try to reinvent the wheel by tearing up the patterns of songwriting. There is a reason our ears tune in to songs on the radio that have structure! I saw a T-shirt one time that read "verse, chorus, verse, chorus, bridge, chorus, chorus," with "worship song" written underneath. It's funny, but in all honesty, we are drawn to structure. That's why so many young people are drawn to a life in the military. I come from an Air Force family, and my dad loved the military life and how it helped shape him as a young man. It gave him an outline and a structure to work in. Songs can become chaotic without framework. Rhyming patterns, arrangement, and instrumentation are all ways we structure a song. Everything in God's incredible creation has order to it. So as we create, let's remember that things with order tend to have beauty! Don't rush it. Have fun, and let every song be an expression of your heart!

Co-writing in Community

When I first moved to Nashville in 2005, it was with my band. I had just gotten married a few months earlier, and we all moved into a four-bedroom place together. I probably wouldn't recommend living with your bandmates if you're a newlywed couple, but we had some fun times too! I had just signed my first publishing deal, which is basically a means of writing songs and getting paid for it. That is, *if* artists and music supervisors like your songs. Up to this point, I had never really written with anyone outside of my band, so when my publisher started to set up co-writes, I was swimming in uncharted waters.

The first writing session was with a guy who had written several hits in country music, and when we first met up, he asked me to show him some of my best unwritten melodies. I did, and he responded by saying, "Do you have any better ones?" Ego shattered. I love the Nelson Mandela quote "I never lose. I either win or learn." That day was a learning experience for me, and I began to see the value in writing with other people.

We all know that community is messy, but it's worth it. The relationships in our lives are placed there for a reason. Following Jesus isn't a solo sport. If you're a worship leader, or on a worship team, that atmosphere is a great place to build community. And worship songwriting is a lot of fun when you do it with those you lead with. But just like relationships, songwriting can get into troubled waters if you don't set some ground rules.

In my house we have our "family values" posted on the wall so that we can see it when we first come in. In case you care, we have five values in the Parks home: Love God, Love each other, Have fun, Be generous, Be grateful. It's the operating system in our home. Every community needs to know the values. And co-writing needs to be done in a family spirit, with a heart to honor one another. "As iron sharpens iron, so a friend sharpens a friend" (Prov. 27:17). Many of us have heard this verse, but what you may not realize is that when metal strikes metal, sparks fly! There's a clashing in sharpening, and that can often happen in a co-writing session.

Songwriting with others can often feel like one person attacking another person's ideas. In my first Nashville session, mentioned earlier, it felt like I was getting beat up. To write songs with friends and fellow worshipers, you need to set a safe zone where everyone has the freedom to share. There's a lot less pressure when you realize that even though every idea may not be used, every idea can be heard. The following are a few tips when it comes to co-writing:

Everyone Bring an Idea

There's nothing worse than showing up to a potluck and missing the memo that you were supposed to bring a food item. Your portion adds to the whole meal, and without it there's a feeling of incompleteness. There's also nothing worse than showing up to write something and no one has brought an idea. Come with a couple ideas to launch off of—whether it's a scripture that's been challenging you, a story in your church that's laced in testimony, or a simple melody that's caught in your head. When multiple people come with multiple ideas, then you can toss them out to the writing group and see which one resonates the most with everyone. I like the language "see what sticks." Then you have a starting line. You'll have to lay down pride, but that's what brings me to the next point.

Hold On to Ideas Loosely

We often say, don't be married to a melody and don't be locked into your lyrics. If you're writing with others, know that you're putting it all on the table in the hopes that the best meal will come out of it. Like a cooking class with different ingredients, one person might bring a lyric or two, while another person might bring a melody that gets used for a chorus. The goal is to come away from the session with something you all love and are proud of.

But when writing worship music, personal pride has no place. It needs to be done in a way that builds and encourages one another. You might think yours is the best lyric since sliced bread, but other people may think it stinks. What you might want to throw away could be the very line that anchors the entire song. Don't wear your emotions on your sleeve when you write. Have a tough skin but keep a soft heart. You can't get offended easily if you want to co-write. I learned that lesson the hard way! And as much as you want your ideas to be honored, champion other people in their ideas!

Write Out of Relationship

A few years ago I was in Colorado Springs on a songwriting retreat. I was one of the new guys in the room, and there were some giants in the faith there! I took a bold step and asked Jennie Lee Riddle to write with me, and as soon as we sat down, Paul Baloche walked into the room. I was floored when he wanted to join our writing session. Here I was with two people I greatly admire in worship songwriting, whose songs I had sung hundreds of times. I wanted to throw out all my best ideas and prove that I belonged in the room, but do you know what happened? We just started talking.

For at least an hour, we shared what God was doing in each of our lives, how He was moving, what areas we were being challenged in, what was happening in our churches, and where our faith was being stretched. After one of the coolest conversations I've ever been a part of, we picked up our guitars and began to write a song called "In the Name of the King." To this day it's one of my favorites, and it happened out of relationship. I'm honored to call Jennie and Paul friends and not just co-writers.

That day I learned that to write an authentic song, you need to start from a place of relationship. Don't rush into the song session; first lay a foundation of friendship. Get to know someone and their story. It's usually out of those stories that a song is born. But even if a song doesn't happen, you can walk away with a lasting relationship. Music has a tendency to tear down walls and unite people from different walks of life. I've had writing sessions that turned into prayer sessions. I've had some of the best friendships spawn from co-writing.

Honor Each Other's Strengths

It's impossible to build a house if you only have plumbers show up to the construction site. Yes, you're going to need pipes and toilets, but you need concrete, drywall, windows, electricity, and more. It takes different skill sets to build a house, with each strength working together to create something. That same mindset is needed to write a song. As I said before, songwriting in its raw form is lyric plus melody. If you don't know which side of that coin is your strong suit, you will after a while. Much like trying different positions on a sports team, you'll find which songwriting lane you run best in.

For the longest time, I thought of myself as a melody guy because I heard melodies all the time. However, once I started getting involved in writing sessions with dozens of other songwriters, they kept calling me a lyric guy. So now I lean heavily into that. I want to have better melody people in the room when I write. It's not a threat to me or what I bring to the table, because it's all working together to craft a song. If you play guitar and someone else plays keys, mix it up. Have multiple instruments in the room and you'll stumble into different worlds of melody.

I also love writing with non-musical people because they can help me keep the songs singable for the average Joe. I enjoy writing with highly gifted singers because if they can't find a harmony, it's back to the drawing board. I've written with drummers who lay down a beat during the session. Producers have the end song in mind and can usually piece together guitar parts or piano lines to help the song get moving in the right direction. Find people who are gifted in areas where you're not, and come away with a much stronger, more well-rounded song.

At the end of the day, if you're writing worship songs or have the desire to, you need to be in it for the right reasons. Honor God, encourage one another, and challenge yourself. I've heard stories of hit songwriters in the pop and country worlds just wanting to write songs for the church to get more royalties. That hurts my heart and I know it grieves the Lord's. I hate to think that Christianity has become an industry to some people. More than likely, if you're writing to simply have a hit, you'll never get one. The writers in the worship landscape who happen to have massive songs are blessed not because they wanted to be famous but because they wanted to make God's name famous. Sure, there are some exceptions, but for the most part, just like any other area of our lives, if God can get it *through* you, God will get it *to* you.

Let songwriting be a weapon in your hand to arm your church with a song. And even if your church is the only one who happens to sing it, that's a pretty amazing thought. Heck, even if you are the only one who sings it, you're still living out that instruction in Psalms. A completely original tune is hitting heaven's atmosphere with a sound of praise. So go ahead and sing a new song!

Closing Thoughts

When Kurtis approached me to add my voice to this incredible book on worship, specifically the chapter on songwriting, I was both humbled and excited to have the opportunity to share thoughts on a topic that is very dear to my heart and a large part of my involvement in Christian ministry. After reading the chapter that he wrote, I am unsure that I can add anything of value as he has covered "singing a new song" in such a balanced, practical, and inspiring way.

What I would share with you is to never forget the sacredness that adorns our privilege to seek the heart of God through the process of writing songs of praise, and the adoration that must be undergirded with truth and grace. When we consider the innumerable hymns, psalms, and spiritual songs that were written as a record of what God was doing in history at the time they were written, we can see our part in the preservation and furtherance of sharing God's story in our time for future generations.

Consider John and Charles Wesley, who, while preaching the glories of God in an open field, were motivated to write the words "O for a thousand tongues to sing my great Redeemer's praise!" Or contemplate the redemptive lyrics of John Newton, a former slave trader turned abolitionist, following his conversion to Christianity: "Amazing grace how sweet the sound that saved a wretch like me." Even in recent years, think of Matt Redman, who, following a decision by his pastor to simplify production elements in lieu of Matt leading worship in the church with an acoustic guitar, would pen such powerful words and call the church to rediscover the heart of worship: "where it's all about You, Jesus."

This intersection of creativity, history, personal experience, and truth creates a powerful testimony of the power and love of God. It has the ability to teach, remind, and call listeners and singing participants to join in faith with a choir past, present, and future whose songs ring eternal and whose subject is enthroned upon those melodies.

It is a sacred privilege at every level to write songs for and about Jesus. Remind yourself of this and it will never become rote or formulaic. It will remain a privilege in your heart, mind, and soul.

Ian Zumback
Songwriter and recording artist, Old Bear Records

CHAPTER 11

The Art of *Selah*

I grew up in a hunting family. My dad comes from a long line of hunters who had lots of land in Pennsylvania. When I was a teenager, our family built a house on seven acres of land in Salem, Virginia, and my brother and I got bows and rifles that year for Christmas. It was something like *Little House on the Prairie* meets *Duck Dynasty*. My brother loved hunting, and he was pretty good at it—except for the time when he nearly cut his hand off while gutting a deer.

I probably would have enjoyed hunting a little more if I wasn't so impatient—also if you didn't have to wake up at 4:30 a.m. to do it. When you go hunting, you have to sit still up in a tree stand, sometimes for hours, waiting for that perfect moment when a deer walks in your path. Then, ever so quietly, you have to prepare the shot without the deer sensing any motion. Then you have to have that perfect aim to take down the enemy. The enemy in this case is an antlered beast of the woods that will provide lots of tasty meals to come. Sorry to the animal lovers reading this, but rest assured we were always responsible and ate every last piece of venison a deer had to offer. To this day, my grandpa's deer jerky is one of my favorite snacks! I was never that great at hunting, and I haven't been one time in the last 15 years. Fishing trips with my son Moses are more my style these days! But those times back in high school in the quiet woods taught me a lesson that I've held onto for many years: sometimes, for the right thing to come along, you have to be still and just wait.

Over time many things have become extinct, from plants and animals to entire civilizations. But one thing is seriously an endangered species in our noisy day and age: silence. In fact, according to acoustic ecologist Gordon Hempton, there may only be 10-12 places left in the United States where you can find complete silence—no traffic noise, no construction cranes, no sirens, and no planes breaking the sound barrier above your head.

For the record, it's on my bucket list to visit the Hoh River Valley in Washington's Olympic National Park. You have to hike three miles into the park, away from the crowds. The crazy thing is that this particular complete realm of silence measures only one square inch! It's getting harder and harder to find places where noise isn't the default language. There's actually a term called "noise pollution." Research has shown that exposure to noise can increase the chances of heart disease and stroke and damage the development of kids' reading skills. For wildlife, noise can result in hearing loss and the inability to hear important natural sounds (like predators) and can harm animals through increased heart and respiration rates and behavioral changes.[1]

Take a Chill Pill

When I was a kid, I worried about a lot of silly things: my bike had a flat tire, our Nintendo was glitching, the girl at school didn't return my love letter (you know, the ones that say "Do you like me?" followed by the box options "yes," "no," or "maybe"). Whatever it was, I'd express my young angst to my parents, to which they'd often reply, "Kurt, take a chill pill!" That phrase became popular in hip-hop culture in the 1980s, but interestingly enough, in the late 1800s there was an actual recipe for a "chill pill." It was a remedy for kids with high fevers, made up of quinine and oil of black pepper! Probably not the tastiest of medicines.

I think sometimes that as our perfect parent, God would want to tell us to take a chill pill. We are a society that is too worried, and it's often about things that aren't worth it. It's in the stillness of His presence that He holds us and wants to help us trust in His goodness. It's in the quiet place that God speaks. When we freak out and worry, it's because somewhere in our hearts, we don't fully trust God. We have a lot on our

1. (https://www.discovery.com/exploration/a-spot-in-washington-is-one-of-only-12-silent-places-left-in-the)

plates, no doubt, but there's nothing we have that God can't handle.

It was a simple song that won the 1989 Grammy for "Song of the Year", "Record of the Year", and "Best Male Pop Vocal Performance." It was also the first acappella song to not only make the Billboard Hot 100 but also to hit number one on that list! One music critic noted it as a "formula for facing life's trials." What song am I talking about? "Don't Worry, Be Happy" by Bobby McFarin. Simple message. Profound implications. It's hard to worry if you're happy, and it's impossible to be happy if you're always worrying.

In His Sermon on the Mount, Jesus tells us:

> Therefore I tell you, do not worry about your life, what you will eat or drink; or about your body, what you will wear. Is not life more than food, and the body more than clothes? Look at the birds of the air; they do not sow or reap or store away in barns, and yet your heavenly Father feeds them. Are you not much more valuable than they? Can any one of you by worrying add a single hour to your life? (Matt. 6:25-27)

It's not our job to worry. It's God's job to take care of us. The word "worry" in Matthew 6 is *merimnao* in Greek. It means to be distracted, to be over-anxious.

I know what you're thinking: *Oh man, Jesus just doesn't get it. He doesn't understand the kind of stress I'm under. He doesn't understand what's happening in the world with unrest, politics, constant shifts in culture, and an unreliable economy.* But let me tell you that Jesus said these words in a culture that was under a lot of oppression, stress, and Roman rule. Scripture tells us that Jesus, while being the Son of God, was also fully man, and He walked in our shoes. Hebrews 4:15 says it like this: "For we do not have a high priest who is unable to empathize with our weaknesses, but we have one who has been tempted in every way, just as we are—yet he did not sin." Jesus gets it. He knows what we're going through. And He says there's a way to overcome.

See, Jesus doesn't just tell us to *not* do something. He tells us to *do* something about it. It's one thing if I just tell you, "Don't take that route. Don't take that street. This road is closed." But if I just leave it at that, I'm not giving you an alternative. I'm just telling you what doesn't work. Jesus always gives us the answer; He gives us the way: it's "Don't worry, but *seek* Him first." "Don't worry" is a dead-end street. "Seek Him first" is the path to life.

This is why it's so important to have time set aside every day to just be in His presence and let your heart become centered on His goodness—and to teach your team, and give space for your church to do the same, to just rest in His arms. How do we simply *be* in His presence? Let me introduce you to the art of *selah*.

Pause and Reflect

Seventy-one times throughout the book of Psalms, there is a word that captures this idea. In fact, it even occurs three times in Habakkuk (the way you pronounce this might just make or break our relationship). *Selah* is a word that even scholars don't quite know the purest translation. The closest meaning that we've come to is "a musical direction toward pausing and reflecting." And if that is the meaning that we mostly agree on, it's something worth leaning into.

David and the other songwriters used this at the end of a verse, and I can only imagine they put it there for the singers, and the readers later on (that's you and me), to not rush the moment. Don't just move on to the next stanza, but process what you just heard. Wrestle with it. Pray through it.

Psalm 3 is a great example of how *selah* points to a reflection. David wrote this particular song while he was on the run not from Saul but from his son Absalom! His own flesh and blood wanted to take his throne, and David was at a point in his life when he didn't want any more fighting, so he gave it up. He was probably contemplating all of the family tension, the chaos of losing a kingdom, and wondering where God's hand was in all of this as he wrote the words in this psalm. And there are three particular *selah* moments, each giving a different reason to stop and meditate.

> O Lord, I have so many enemies;
> so many are against me.
> So many are saying,
> "God will never rescue him!" *Selah*

Stop, collaborate, and listen! (Any Vanilla Ice fans out there?) David was pondering the situation he was in—thinking about all the haters, and realizing he had quite a few people who were against him in a massive conspiracy to take his kingdom.

> But you, O Lord, are a shield around me;
>> you are my glory, the one who holds my head high.
> I cried out to the Lord,
>> and he answered me from his holy mountain. *Selah*

Here David was recognizing that the one constant throughout all the chaos was the Lord. He never left him and never abandoned him. He was the God who answers! The *selah* happens one last time after the last verse of this psalm: "Victory comes from you, O Lord. May you bless your people. *Selah*."

David knew that his future was in the hands of God. The God who gave him victory in the pasture, on the battlefield, and as a king of Israel, would be able to do it again. And sure enough, David returned to the throne as king after his army defeated Absalom.

Busy Ain't Better

You want to know my favorite ride these days at a water park? While most kids make a dash for the zip lines and water slides, I head straight for the lazy river. I don't even know if that classifies as a ride, but something about just chilling in a tube as the current takes me for a spin is appealing to me these days. I guess that makes me a bit of an old man. Don't worry, I'm not walking around in socks and sandals just yet. But did you know that one definition of the word "lazy" is simply "slow-moving"? I am by no means advocating idleness, but I think in our ever-rushed, nonstop busy culture of hurry, we need some slow moving.

Here's some food for thought: Jesus was never in a hurry! One of my mentors reminded me of that when we were in our pre-launch phase of church planting. I felt like I had to meet a million people, fill my days with fundraising talks and strategy sessions, and connect with local pastors—all while maintaining my role as husband, dad, provider, and most importantly Jesus follower. Jesus, without a doubt the greatest example of perfect ministry, never hurried. Even when He found out that one of His best friends, Lazarus, was on his deathbed, Jesus took a couple of days to get around to visiting. Why? Because He knew something most of us never figure out in this lifetime: God has no limits to His power and His wisdom, including the limits of time and space.

In his book *The Ruthless Elimination of Hurry,* John Mark Comer writes, "Not only does hurry keep us from the love, joy, and peace of the kingdom of God—the very core of what all human beings crave—but it also keeps us from God himself simply by stealing our attention. And with hurry, we always lose more than we gain." *Selah.*

Corrie ten Boom once said, "If the devil can't make you bad, he'll make you busy!" If that's not a convicting statement, then I don't know what is. So many of us are just too busy. We stack up our schedules, and then if we have any time left we give it to God. As a worship leader on staff at a church, you can be just as guilty of busyness as a person who works in the corporate world. And coffee doesn't help! Rehearsals on rehearsals, shifting through set lists, recording tracks, and other tasks are necessary—but don't get lost in them.

I remember a season during my time as a worship pastor when I was so busy with *things* that I lost a lot of time with *people.* Relationships are the currency of the Kingdom, and we need to always put people as priority. And the relationship that stands above every other in importance is the one you have with your heavenly Father. It's so crucial to spend time with God in the rhythm of our lives and create those *selah* moments when we simply sit or stand in His presence and be still. We live in a "go, go, go" culture where if we're not moving, then we're not productive. Yet I've seen in my personal relationship with Christ that when I'm still in His presence, He speaks. And it's after hearing His voice, the gentle whisper of the Spirit, that I can then move again, with greater purpose than before. You know the verse: "Be still and know that I am God" (Ps. 46:10). There are a few *selahs* throughout that chapter as well.

Being still is so hard. My brother had the nickname "Worm" because he could never sit still during a meal or in class. It's not easy to rest or reflect. But we have to create those moments for space and margin where the Lord can do soul work on us. We tend to think that if we're not "doing something," then we're not "becoming anything." We are not human doings; we're human beings. We need to just *be* with the Father.

As worship leaders, don't buy into the lie that you have to be busy all the time. So many of us will post all of this flash on social media, trying to find validation and affirmation through all of the cool stuff that we're doing. But it only feeds the lie that you're not good if you're not busy. Spend time with the Lord before you go about your day. Ask God to guide you and lead you and to highlight moments when you need to lean in. Find the strength and confidence you need for the day in God alone. I love this verse that a pastor friend recently encouraged me with:

> This is what the Sovereign Lord,
>   the Holy One of Israel, says:
> "Only in returning to me
>   and resting in me will you be saved.
> In quietness and confidence is your strength.
>   But you would have none of it."
> (Isaiah 30:15, NLT)

"In quietness and confidence is your strength." Those two concepts seem to be polar opposites, but there is a confidence (translated here into "trust") that comes from resting, returning, and being still. Augustine said, "Our hearts are restless until they rest in you." If you find yourself constantly overwhelmed with life, *selah*.

Hey Man, Listen

One of my favorite people to talk with is Joshua Symonette. Former NFL linebacker, brilliant preacher, and now a church planter, he's a dude with much experience and wisdom. He usually starts off our conversations with "Hey man, listen." Listening is a spiritual discipline. There's a term called "active listening" where you are intentionally leaning in to the other person involved in the conversation, completely immersed in their story, their life. Andy Stanley encourages us to "listen to understand, and not just listen to reply." In your prayer life, who does most of the talking—you or God? In your rehearsals, is it only your voice that gets heard, or do others feel like they're invited to the table? Part of the beauty in silence and *selah* is that it forces us to become better listeners. I've learned to be still even in the presence of God and to let Him do the talking.

Stop and Consider

For the last decade I've made a practice of reading through the Bible in a year. The YouVersion app makes it simple, and I have to be honest, I take advantage of the audio version as much as I can. It makes driving an intentional Bible study, every time in the car! But every year, when I get to the book of Job, I get a little bummed. Job had a rough go of it. If you're in a down mood, I wouldn't recommend reading the story of Job. Actually, it could be the *perfect* book to read! You'll see that you don't have it that bad, but it's a tough story to swallow. The overall theme shows us that even when life is completely in the dumps, God is with you. Even when it seems like all is lost, there is more. There are so many gold nuggets in the book of Job, but one of my favorite verses is Job 37:14: "Listen to this, Job; stop and consider God's wonders."

When was the last time you stopped and considered all the miracles that God has done in your life? His wondrous workings all around you? If we don't take inventory of His work in our lives, it can be easy to focus on the struggle. This is why the Israelites built altars. It gave them a physical reminder of the battles that God won. I'm sure it also built the faith of those who didn't witness the victory firsthand, as they saw a reminder of God's goodness and promise to generations past. Stop and consider what He's brought you through, and give Him praise. *Selah* helps you focus on His wonder. *Selah* is stopping and considering.

Sometimes you just need to get out of your normal habitat to appreciate the vastness of God. I love to get out into nature on a regular basis. It's one way that I *selah*. For a couple summers in a row, I had the opportunity to lead worship for a youth camp in Colorado at Lake Navajo. During the week we took hiking trips in the mountains, alongside crystal clear rivers. It was a picture of the majestic God who paints pictures in the sky and speaks light into existence. When you see how *big* our God is, you realize how *small* your battles are. It's all about perspective. That's not to minimize your pain or struggle. It's to encourage you that there's nothing God can't handle. As Psalm 8 tells us, the same God who created the oceans knows you by name, and He is mindful of you (see v. 4).

As worship leaders, we often sing songs that talk about the majesty and splendor of God's creation, and yet we rarely make the effort to go out and experience it. When you hike a mountain, you get a better appreciation for Psalm 121. When you row down a river, you see Psalm 46:4 in a new light. When you hike through a canyon, you'll read Psalm 23 through fresh eyes. Go out and soak in the beauty of creation.

Come to Me

When we first started Bridges Nashville, I went through an intense role transition. For seven years I had been on staff as the worship pastor and director at National Community Church. Now, planting a church, I was in a completely different lane as a lead pastor. In the shift, I learned to retreat and get alone with God in a new way. My friend David, who eventually would join our staff, said to me, "Don't come to God as a pastor; come to Him as a son." That changed the way I prayed. It changed the way I viewed myself. I pray it shapes the way you view yourself today. God doesn't value you because of anything you *do*; He values you because of who you *are*—His son, His daughter. According to Romans 8:15, we have been adopted into the family of God. How amazing is that? In the stillness of His presence, as you meditate on His goodness, know that you are in the arms of the Father. Let Him shape your identity in the quiet place.

Make Space

One of my go-to musical artists is the band Sigur Ros. In my opinion, they have some of the most inspiring and creative music in the world. They create a landscape of atmospheric music that takes you to another world. I believe that as worship teams and leaders, when we lead our congregations in musical worship, we are getting a glimpse of another world. Worship is what happens in heaven 24/7.

Then a voice came from the throne, saying:

> "Praise our God,
>   all you his servants,
> you who fear him,
>   both great and small!"
> Then I heard what sounded like a great multitude, like the roar
> of rushing waters and like loud peals of thunder, shouting:
> "Hallelujah!
>   For our Lord God Almighty reigns."
> (Rev. 19:5-6)

Most of the scriptures that give insight to heaven speak about worship. I like to think that wherever we walk in eternity will have a soundtrack to it. We'll live in a suspended *selah*. In our church gatherings, during musical worship, I believe it's important to have moments of silence, moments when no words are being sung, and moments when a bed of music provides a soundtrack to prayer. As I said in an earlier chapter, in our worship service at Bridges, we have a *selah* moment every time we gather, when the band just plays instrumentally out of our communion song. We show Bible verses about His peace, power, and presence on our screens. Our prayer team is standing in the wings, at the ready to pray for people. Some of the congregation stand, some kneel, others sit at their tables and open up the Scriptures. It's simply a time of being unrushed in the presence of almighty God. Maybe there's a line from the message that is challenging someone. Maybe there's a particular lyric from a worship song that is ministering to someone.

Our *selah* is an intentional time of letting the sanctuary actually become a sanctuary! It's usually less than five minutes long, but that is a lifetime in today's hurried culture. It's a rhythm that people find refreshing in our service, and it's one of my favorite parts of Sunday. I'd encourage you to find moments both corporately as the Church to rest in His presence and in your personal life to get alone and *selah*. I want to close this chapter with lyrics from a worship song I led a lot in my college days at Campus Crusade for Christ:

> In the secret in the quiet place
> In the stillness you are there
> In the secret in the quiet hour
> I wait only for you
> 'Cause I want to know you more
> ("In the Secret" by Andy Park)

Learn to just *be* in His presence, and help others to do the same. That's part of pastoring and leading worship—giving your team and church the tools to go deeper in their everyday lives with Jesus.

Closing Thought

I have to admit, I haven't always loved discipline. In fact, for many years I ran from it. Maybe it's the creative in me. Maybe it's the flesh. But there's something about being desperate that makes you open to finding a new way. And that's exactly what happened to me.

I was going through a tough season, and a dear friend of mine

talked me into taking a class on two-way journaling. I went reluctantly. Honestly, I had a fear of journaling since my sister broke into my diaries. That's partly why I started writing my feelings into songs in the first place! But again, I was desperate.

I learned through this beautiful community that I could write out my thoughts, prayers, meditations of scripture, and questions, and then listen and give God room to speak. I didn't know that He actually would, but He did! One day in particular, He began speaking to me about bread. I saw a picture of Jesus pulling a freshly baked loaf of bread out of a brick oven with a wooden paddle. On the bread was written the word "intimacy." I heard Him say that I had been spiritually gluten-free, picking and choosing which bread I was going to eat, when all the while, everything He gave me was meant to bring me closer to Him. He reminded me of the story of the Israelites with the manna. There was a reason they were given this bread daily and in the morning. I sensed the Lord was calling me to manna mornings too.

For the next several months, I experienced something I never had before. At about 5:30 a.m. every morning, I would smell freshly baked bread. I literally couldn't go back to sleep because it smelled so *good*. It drew me in, and I couldn't hold myself back from going downstairs to spend time with God by reading my Bible, psalming (singing the psalms), and two-way journaling.

After a couple of months, I stopped smelling the bread. But I still wake up to get it every day. I'll never go hungry again. While the discipline does cost me something, I know now that what I get in return is so much more. There is bread waiting for you too!

Krissy Nordhoff
Songwriter, teacher, and author; founder, Brave Worship

Scan the QR code for a closing thought with KP.

Acknowledgments

I have to give a ton of props to the team that made this book a reality. To every worship leader and artist who contributed to the chapters in this book, your hearts and voices are gifts to the Kingdom of God.

Greg Johnson at WordServe Literary, you are not only an agent but an advocate and a friend. Thank you for believing in this idea and message when others just dismissed it. Robert Walker at The Core Media Group, you championed this thing from the start and gave it your all. Grateful to have you as a friend and peer. Nadia Guy, thank you for putting your heart into the editing process. Riley Flynn, your eye for design is only matched by your heart of gold bro! You made this not just a book cover, but a complete branding!

Thank you to my Bridges Nashville family. You have been an honor to pastor, to lead, and to grow with. PD, Sara, Patrick, and Delaney—you are the best staff to do ministry with! Cordell and Luke, your passion to grow and sow is inspiring. Pastor Adonis, the baton is in your hands! I can't wait to see what comes NEXT!

Thanks to the pastors in my life who are some of the best examples of Christ on this planet. Mark Batterson, your champion spirit makes me want to pay everything forward. Thanks for your generosity and example that you've set for all these years! Stephen Blandino, thanks for the constant support, belief, and connections to make this book happen! Bryan Briggs, you make ministry fun, and I always believe the best is yet to come when I'm around you! Dad (Terry Parks), thanks for always picking up the phone and for speaking life into me, usually with a funny story behind it.

Thanks to my family for being in my corner and for giving me a reason to never stop moving forward. Sarah, your love is proof that God is good. You are my best friend and my greatest love. Norah and Mo, you give me my greatest role in life—dad! I love you so much.

TO JOIN THE WORSHIPOLOGY ONLINE COACHING COMMUNITY, PLEASE VISIT WWW.KURTISPARKS.COM/ WORSHIPOLOGY

TO BOOK KURTIS TO SPEAK OR LEAD WORSHIP, PLEASE VISIT WWW.KURTISPARKS.COM